T0246451

EXPLORERS

NORTON
SHORTS

EXPLORERS

A New History

MATTHEW LOCKWOOD

W. W. NORTON & COMPANY
Independent Publishers Since 1923

Manufacturing by Lakeside Book Company
Production manager: Delaney Adams

ISBN: 978-1-324-07387-1

W. W. Norton & Company, Inc.
500 Fifth Avenue, New York, NY 10110
www.wwnorton.com

W. W. Norton & Company Ltd.
15 Carlisle Street, London W1D 3BS

10 9 8 7 6 5 4 3 2 1

For my brothers: Jack, Kaleb, John, Joey, and Josh

CONTENTS

EXPLORERS

THE NEW EXPLORERS

——

E XPLORERS HAVE HAD a stubborn and enduring legacy. Most of us still want to believe that there are people who risk their lives in pursuit of nothing more than knowledge and adventure, who journey into unknown corners of the world simply to see what might be seen. Many still want heroes. And thus, the heroic image of the explorer endures in our popular culture, from novels to the screen: a valiant captain astride the deck of a storm-tossed ship, eyes fixed on the world he (it is usually he) hopes to find beyond the gale; a khaki-clad adventurer hacking his way through a tangled jungle in quest of some long lost city; a mountaineer inching his way across a perilous chasm, a thin rope all that separates survival and disaster.

Such depictions often lie in an uncomfortable juxtaposition with what we know about the entanglement of exploration and imperialism, and it is tempting to discard the terms "discovery" and "exploration" altogether, to consign studies of explorers to the dustbin of history. But if we discard the history of exploration, we discard a vital element of the human story along with it, a story that transcends culture, ethnicity, gender, and geography. Indeed, it is impossible to understand the history of humanity or fully comprehend the human condition without understanding the universal impulse to explore. People of every background imagine new worlds. People from every corner of the globe search for the unknown, seeking out the unfamiliar and trying to understand it.

Too often, though, our narratives of the past have been circumscribed. The stories became repeated until they were almost parodies: Columbus spying flecks of green among the endless blue on the western horizon, just as his weary crew has begun to abandon all hope of ever seeing dry land again; "Stout Cortez" gazing out at the vast Pacific, waiting to see, in the immortal words of John Keats, what new worlds might "swim into his ken"; Lewis and Clark pushing through the brush to see the mighty Columbia River guiding their expedition and their country to the promise of the Pacific; a Welsh reporter and a Scottish missionary clasping hands deep in Equatorial Africa, with the all-too-casual salutation, "Dr. Livingstone, I presume." These tales fueled adventure stories retold and resold for centuries—and they also obscured the truth about exploration: its costs, its challenges, and its participants.

In this book, I'll place the story of the Moroccan explorer Ibn Battuta alongside the story of his Venetian contemporary Marco Polo, and the story of the Chinese admiral Zheng He alongside the story of the Portuguese navigator Vasco da Gama, reconsidering what it means to be an explorer and what qualifies as discovery. But ultimately I hope to go further: to reimagine the idea of exploration itself.

We tend to think of explorers, unlike mere travelers, as selfless figures who voyage in pursuit of knowledge and adventure. George Mallory's famous explanation for his attempt to climb Mount

Everest—"because it's there"—has become the classic cri de coeur of the noble-minded explorer. But of course, exploration has always been a matter of competing motivations. Curiosity and adventure have their place, but so do economic interest, political calculation, ego, social pressure, and sheer necessity. When Henry Morton Stanley set off across Africa in search of the missing Dr. Livingstone in 1871, his motivation was not merely selfless rescue: Stanley hoped to bury the stigma of his illegitimate birth by making his name as a journalist and to leverage his knowledge of the African interior to make his fortune. Yet, recognizing the complex motivations that drove discovery—rather than ascribing them to limited, narrow circumstances—allows us to see a whole new set of stories as those of explorers. The cast of adventurers I will follow in this short book embarked on discovery for a host of reasons. Some voyaged out of need, escaping bondage, war, and famine in search of prosperity and peace. Others traveled as captives or because the appearance of a new, foreign power on their doorstep required a recalibration of their political geography. Still others, like Woollarawarre Bennelong, the Eora leader who traveled to England, set out because they wished to see what lay on the other side of an ocean.

This book takes seriously the stories of famed explorers like Captain Cook and Robert Peary, whose voyages of discovery helped shape how we understand our world. But it does so alongside the stories of a new cast of adventurers every bit as daring and adventurous as the more familiar figures of old. We'll meet Gudrid Far-Traveler, the Viking woman who helped found the first European settlement in the Americas, and the medieval Uyghur monk Rabban Bar Sauma, the first person from China to visit Rome and Paris. We'll follow the journey of the African traveler Yasuke from his home in East Africa to India and Japan, where he became a confidant of the powerful daimyo Oda Nobunaga, and trace the many expeditions of the caravan leader Ghulam Rassul Galwan through the Himalayas. We'll learn about a young English mother named Mary Wortley Montagu, who learned the secrets of smallpox inoculation from the female practitioners of the Ottoman Empire, and John Edmonstone, who escaped slavery in Guiana to set up a taxidermy shop in Glasgow, where he taught a young Charles Darwin the science of animal preservation. We'll encounter the Indian traveler Dean Mahomet, the Scottish explorer Mungo Park, and the American paleontologist Roy Chapman Andrews. Their stories will take us through every age and to every corner of the globe, from the

BEN-NIL-LONG IN HIS EUROPEAN DRESS.
Engraved for the History of New South Wales.

With his protégé Yemmerrawanne, Woollarawarre Bennelong (1764–1813), of the Eora people of Port Jackson, was the first Aboriginal Australian to explore Europe. His arrival in England in 1793 caused considerable excitement, resulting in numerous portraits, most depicting him in European clothes. (Album/British Library/Alamy Stock Photo)

Epic of Gilgamesh in 2100 BCE to the migrant pathfinders on the Rio Grande in the present day—until a new history of exploration begins to emerge.

Discovery is not unidirectional and never belongs to a single group of people. When the Eora leader Bennelong's ship docked at Falmouth in 1793, didn't he discover England for the Indigenous peoples of Australia just as Captain Cook had discovered Australia for the English some twenty years before? Fugitives from slavery, the panoply of immigrants who fostered the notion of "the American dream," the Jamaican migrants who transformed Britain in the 1950s, the Black Southerners seeking better lives in the North in the Great Migration—don't they all belong in the pantheon of great explorers? All were explorers in every way that matters.

Not for a moment do I wish to excuse or explain away the tragedy, the trauma, or the horrors that undergirded some of these journeys. I wish instead to recover the extraordinary humanity displayed in the journeys of these explorers. Need and necessity, coercion and violence conditioned the experience of migrants, fugitive slaves, and Indigenous ambassadors, guides, and porters, but they were not the sum total of that experience. It is of course vital to understand the driving factors of want and force, the cruelty of the systems that determined the simple ability to stay home. But let us not rob these explorers of their agency or flatten their experiences.

What follows is a story of exploration, of imagination and wonder, curiosity, connection, and exchange, with old adventurers and overlooked explorers placed side by side. These stories are only a few of the millions of other stories told and untold, of explorers known and unknown, whose stories have been lost, casualties of time or the inequities of race and class that have silenced far too many voices for far too long. Others can only be recovered by reading standard accounts of exploration against the grain, listening for the echoes of overlooked explorers they contain and amplifying those whispers. The forgotten explorers are there, in every fugitive slave narrative, in every migrant letter home, and in every reference to guides and porters. They can be recovered. We only need to look. Only by reimagining what it means to be an explorer, by taking seriously the lives of *all* who explore, can we hope to fully understand a basic human need: to seek to know the world.

CHAPTER 1

IMAGINING

———

EVERY JOURNEY BEGINS in the imagination. From the first of the *Homo sapiens* to set out from the Great Rift Valley to the first human to step out onto the surface of the moon, every act of exploration has taken hold in the adventurer's mind before it is accomplished. Human exploration began in prehistory, as far back as 300,000 BCE, when the first humans left their homes in East Africa and set out across first Africa and then Eurasia. Over the next 300,000 years, the human family spread out across the far reaches of the globe. The earliest accounts of exploration that emerged in the ancient world—handed down to us in myths and epics told and retold around the fire for generations before they were written down—carry fragmentary memories of this first age of discovery. Myths of migration and exploration—suggesting that we, our human family, began in another place before we came to this one; or that siblings went different ways; or that someone was cast out to make a new life elsewhere; or that a traveler from a far-off place was taken in—helped to weaken geographic distinctions between human groups and inspired curiosity about the outside

world. Imagination thus spurred diffusion in the earliest millennia
of human history, but it also inspired constant acts of reconvergence.
The threads of the human web stretched near to breaking, but connections between distant populations, however faint, remained.

"THERE WAS A MAN who saw the deep, the bedrock of the land,
who knew the ways and learned all things." So opens the *Epic of
Gilgamesh*, the world's oldest written story, the earliest fragments of
which date to 2100 BCE. The written record of human civilization
thus begins with an explorer, the hero-king of the Sumerian city
of Uruk who "sought out rulers everywhere and came to grasp all

*Like many of the earliest stories
to survive from antiquity, the*
Epic of Gilgamesh *tells of a
voyage into unknown lands.*
(The Metropolitan Museum of Art,
New York; Rogers Fund, 1959)

wisdom in the world. He discovered a secret, revealed a hidden matter and brought home a story from before the Flood. He came back
from far roads exhausted but at peace, as he set down all his trials on
a slab of stone."

The Hopi people of the American Southwest also tell an exploration tale of their origins, beginning with a flood. After their home
in the Third World was drowned, the Hopi's ancestors were guided
east across an ocean by the Spider Grandmother until they arrived
on the mountainous shore of our present Fourth World. But their
long journey had just begun. For generations they wandered across
a vast and inhospitable land, dividing into smaller groups and clans
along the way. They traveled to the four corners of the world, unable
to find a suitable place to rest. In the far north, they found a land of
ice and snow, but the "Back Door" that led out of the Fourth World
was closed. Only when they reached northeast Arizona did they find
their true home.

Farther east, the Choctaw tell similar tales of their people's
origins. The land of their forefathers far to the west had withered
and died, forcing two brothers named Chata and Chicksah to lead
their people east, carrying the bones of their ancestors with them.
Each night when they camped, they placed a magical staff in the
ground. Each morning it tilted in the direction they were to travel.
One morning, after ages of ceaseless wandering, they found the staff
standing straight in the ground, indicating that this was the place
where their ancestors could be laid to rest and a new civilization
could begin.

To the south, Aztec origin stories tell of a long journey through
the deserts of Mexico from Aztlán, the mythical homeland of the
Nahua people somewhere in the north. Indeed, the name Aztec

comes from the word *Astekah*, "people of Aztlan." Across the Atlantic, another people crossed another desert to reach the promised land and begin anew. In the book of Exodus, the Torah tells of the Jewish people's flight from slavery in Egypt, their weary years of wandering in the desert, and their eventual arrival in Canaan. On Rapa Nui (Easter Island), one of the most remote outposts of humanity, oral histories recount the legendary first settler of the island, Hotu Matu'a, who sailed from his mythical home island of Hiva ("far-away island") in search of a new island promised to him in a dream.

Similar figures and sagas litter the earliest stories of countless cultures. Homer's *Odyssey*, one of the founding documents of the Western literary tradition, takes up many of the same themes, following its namesake Odysseus on his ten-year journey from the siege of Troy, through strange island worlds populated by lotus-eaters, cannibals, and cyclops, to his home in Greece. "Tell me, O muse," the poem begins, "of the ingenious hero who travelled far and wide. . . . Many cities did he visit, and many were the nations with whose manners and customs he was acquainted." The legendary figures of ancient times were often explorers, their most glorious deeds acts of exploration.

According to the Mahāvaṃsa, the Sri Lankan chronicle composed in the fifth century and based on earlier annals kept by the Buddhist monks of the Anuradhapura Maha Viharaya monastery, the Sinhalese people who now rule Sri Lanka first arrived on the island around 500 BCE. They were followers of the legendary Prince Vijaya, whose ancestors came from Bengal, in India. Vijaya had risen to become the ruler of a prosperous Indian kingdom before being driven into exile by his enemies. Searching for a place of refuge, Vijaya and his seven hundred followers wandered south through the Indian subcontinent until they crossed Palk Strait to Sri Lanka, following in the footsteps of the Buddha himself, who the Mahāvaṃsa recorded had recently traveled to Sri Lanka to pave the way by expelling the yakka (demons) who inhabited the island.

Many centuries later, even as cities swelled into empires, when people imagined their own origins, they likewise thought in terms of exploration. Writing in the first century BCE, the Roman poet Virgil framed the foundation of Rome around the voyage of Aeneas, legendary son of a Trojan prince and the goddess Venus, who survived the fall of his native Troy only to wander for years before arriving in Italy to found the city that would one day become Rome. Several early works of British history, including Geoffrey of Monmouth's influential *Historia Regum Britanniae*, trace British origins back to Aeneas's grandson Brutus, who journeyed to the far-off land of Albion, where he defeated the giants that inhabited the island and peopled it with his progeny. In other versions of the story, Brutus is also descended from one of the sons of Noah, merging classical accounts of civilization with the Abrahamic tradition of human settlement after a voyage across a flooded world.

In all of these origin stories, we can hear the faint echo of an even older journey, the long voyage that brought our earliest human ancestors out of the Rift Valley in East Africa and across the surface of the world. The story of humanity begins with a journey, and the earliest stories people told of their history were stories of exploration. The Hopi story of the "Back Door" in the icy north perhaps recalls the Bering Land Bridge that might have brought their ancestors from Asia to the Americas thousands of years earlier. The Rapa Nui myth of Hotu Matu'a contains the memory of the historic Polynesian migration to the far-flung islands of the South Pacific.

Foundational myths of explorers and exploration continued to be important well into the period of more formally recorded history. Mansa Musa, ruler of the fabulously wealthy Mali Empire in West Africa, explained the origins of his own rule through a story of an expedition of discovery. According to the Arab historian al-Umari, in 1324, while in Cairo on his way to Mecca for the hajj (a pilgrimage perhaps inspired by his people's remarkable history of exploration), Musa told an Egyptian official that he had come to the throne after his predecessor mounted an expedition to sail into the Atlantic to see if, like the great river Niger, it had another bank:

> The ruler who preceded me did not believe that it was impossible to reach the extremity of the ocean that encircles the earth . . . and wanted to reach that (end). . . . He ordered two thousand boats to be equipped for him and for his men, and one thousand more for water and victuals . . . [and] departed with his men on the ocean trip, never to return.

Across civilizations, origins and heroes are passed down through tales of exploration. Exploration and storytelling are inextricably intertwined.

EARLY HISTORICAL EXPLORERS remain figures shrouded in mystery, occupying a middle ground between legendary heroes like Gilgamesh and the well-recorded later lives of the everyday merchants, ambassadors, and pilgrims, who wrote down the stories of their travels in the Middle Ages. What survives of their voyages are hints and vague allusions in the works of later authors, second- and thirdhand stories in which the shreds of truth mingle with the mythological and the fantastic. In the fifth century BCE, a Carthaginian captain named Hanno is said to have sailed from Libya with a fleet of sixty ships through the Strait of Gibraltar and south along the Atlantic coast of Africa until he reached a land of volcanoes and gorillas. But all that remains of his account is a partial Greek translation of the original Punic text. Scholars have been left to guess just how far he traveled, whether all the way to Cameroon, or perhaps only as far as Morocco. Roman writers later described another fifth-century Carthaginian named Himilco, who sailed to northern Europe, encountering sea monsters and what seems to be the seaweed of the Sargasso Sea far out in the Atlantic. Himilco's voyage remains impossible to confirm, but the knowledge of the mid-Atlantic that his story reveals is genuine.

A century later, an explorer from the Greek colony at Marseilles named Phytheas circumnavigated the British Isles and penetrated deep into the Baltic Sea. He was the first writer to mention Scotland, to tell of polar ice, and to describe the firsthand experience of the land of the midnight sun. Like Hanno and Himilco, however, Phytheas's original text only survives in excerpts and paraphrases in the works of later authors. The same is true of the Chinese diplomat Zhang Qian, who was dispatched to Central Asia by Han dynasty emperor Wu in 138 BCE. His journey helped to inaugurate a new era of interconnection in Asia that saw the first flourishing of the famous overland trade network that linked China to India, the Middle East, and the Mediterranean, later called the Silk Road. The truth of his travels is not in question, but his personality, vision, and voice remain a mystery. His journey only survives in the history compiled by his contemporary, Sima Qian.

One of the first explorers to leave a firsthand account of his journey that survives was the Buddhist monk Faxian. In 399 CE, at the age of sixty, Faxian and nine other monks left their monastery in Chang'an (modern Xi'an) in central China and set out on a pilgrimage to India in search of Buddhist texts not available in China. It was a grueling journey on foot across the Gobi Desert, where the only sight other than the "river of sand" was the "dry bones of the dead," and over the high passes of the Himalayas "among the hills and cold," where nothing grew and dragons "spit forth poisonous winds" so bitter that Faxian could not speak. The monks crossed the wide Indus into India, the land of Buddha's birth, where they visited temples and shrines, beheld relics of the Buddha, and walked in his blessed footsteps. Faxian eventually traveled all the way down the Ganges to the religious center of Varanasi and on to Pataliputra, modern Patna. It was all a strange new world for Faxian, but in no way a lesser one. For Faxian, India was the true "Middle Kingdom," the center of the universe. China, which proudly claimed the title for itself, was for him a "border-land." (Such talk would outrage many readers back home in China, but seen through the Buddhist lens, India was the center of the universe.)

Through his account of his travels, first transmitted orally to his fellow monks, then written down in the annals of Buddhist heroes and read across China, Faxian helped to alter China's worldview, decentering his homeland and situating it within a wider world. In so doing, he encouraged curiosity and inquiry and inspired generations of explorers to follow his lead. In Faxian we see, perhaps for the first time, how stories of exploration told from the perspective of the explorer have the power to change the world.

But even when firsthand records survive, early accounts of explorers often veer into legend. In some cases, the explorers become legends themselves. In 629 CE, another Buddhist monk named Xuanzang left China to see the land of the Buddha. Born in Chenliu, Henan Province, in 602 CE, Xuanzang entered a monastery in Sichuan, where he became obsessed with tracking down and collecting original Buddhist scriptures from India. In the process, he learned about the journey of Faxian and became determined to follow his example. Like his predecessor, Xuanzang traveled across the great western deserts and climbed the towering passes of the Himalayas before staggering out, exhausted, onto the Gangeatic plain. At the celebrated Nalanda monastery in Bihar, he at last found what he was looking for, plentiful Sanskrit texts and a mentor, the famous monk Śīlabhadra.

When Xuanzang returned to China in 645, he brought with him twenty packhorses worth of scriptures and a treasure trove of tales about the giant stone Buddhas of Bamiyan in Afghanistan (later destroyed by the Taliban), the workings of the caste system in India, and a fantastical race of dragon men in the high Himalayas. His knowledge of the outside world, real and imagined, transformed Xuanzang from an obscure young monk into a revered figure. With the emperor's backing, he established a translation center at Chang'an that drew students and scholars from across Asia, binding the world closer together and spreading his own name in the process. As his fame grew, some of his fellow monks, at the emperor's insistence, recorded Xuanzang's account of his voyage for posterity, the *Great Tang Records on the Western Regions*.

Xuanzang's journey continued even after his death in 664. His image can be found in temples from Taiwan to Dunhuang, in western China, and his relics are still claimed by India, China, and Japan. Over the centuries, his journey became the inspiration for plays, popular literature, and traveling storytellers. Before long, they became a staple of Chinese culture, increasingly fictionalized as the years passed. By the time of the Ming dynasty in the sixteenth century, life and legend had merged so completely that the real Xuanzang had become the fictional Tang Sanzang, hero of the beloved 1592 novel *Journey to the West*. Today, that story of a wandering monk and his four disciples, including the hugely popular Monkey King, Sun Wukong, continues to appear in popular culture, from *Dragon Ball* to Marvel and DC Comics. But even after Xuanzang's story became subsumed in the legend of Tang Sanzang, the values he represented—openness, curiosity, adventure, exchange—lived on to influence generations of Chinese, Japanese, and Korean readers to look upon the world as a place worthy of exploration.

EXPLORATION AND MYTHMAKING were often so intertwined that genuine accounts of discovery were sometimes dismissed as mere fables. This was doubly true in the case of two of the first Europeans to set foot in the Americas. Born in Iceland around 980 CE, Gudrid Far-Traveler was the descendant of the Scandinavian explorers who had crossed the North Sea in the 700s–800s to settle the islands of the far north Atlantic: the Faroe Islands, the Shetlands, Orkney, and Iceland. When Gudrid was a young woman, she accompanied her father on the expedition led by the notorious Erik the Red that established the first Norse settlement in Greenland. With North America near at hand, and winds and currents favorable for sailing farther west and south, it was not long before sailors began returning to the Greenland settlement with tales of a verdant land in the direction of the setting sun. It was Erik's elder son Leif Erikson who led the first Norse expedition to make landfall in the Americas around the year 1000.

Gudrid's husband Thorstein was Leif's younger brother, so Gudrid had planned to join Leif's second expedition to the place he called Vinland (after the wild grapes he noticed growing onshore). But shortly before Gudrid was set to sail, her husband died. With her sights still fixed beyond the horizon, Gudrid chose a prominent merchant named Thorfinn Karlsefni as her second husband and wasted no time urging him to outfit his own expedition. Together, they would help create the first permanent European settlement in North America in what is now Newfoundland, Canada. There, Gudrid gave birth to a son, Snorri, who became the first child of European descent to be born in the Americas.

Gudrid was not the only Viking woman with interests in exploration. She was joined in the Newfoundland settlement by Leif Erikson's tough-minded sister, Freydís Eiríksdóttir, who arrived in America as a full partner in the settlement venture and the undisputed leader of a party of more than thirty men. When conflict broke out between the Norse interlopers and the *skræling*, the Indigenous people of the region (likely either the ancestors of the Beothuk or the Thule, the ancestors of the Inuit), it was Freydís who led the fight, despite being six months pregnant. Furious at the timidity of the settlement's men, she admonished them for their cowardice, picked up a sword, and rallied the settlers to her. Unlacing her tunic, she beat her bare breast with her sword until the attackers fled. Her bold action in the face of danger would make her a legendary model of female strength, though the two surviving accounts of her life in America differ in their descriptions of her. In *Saga of the Greenlanders*, Freydís is a warning of the dangers of headstrong women; in *Saga of Erik the Red*, she is the personification of maternal bravery and sacrifice. In both, though, the story of her voyage held lasting power.

Gudrid and Freydís both abandoned the Vinland settlement when Indigenous resistance to their presence became too fierce. Freydís returned to Greenland, where a Norse settlement would limp on for another four centuries as the farthest outpost of European settlement. Gudrid settled back in Iceland with her son Snorri, converted to Christianity, and, her thirst for travel still unquenched, made the long pilgrimage to Rome. Both women became legendary figures in their native land, their history eventually elided with the myths that surrounded them. For almost one thousand years, their actual existence was widely dismissed. Indeed, the very fact that two women helped to lead the first European expeditions to the Americas was often interpreted by scholars as evidence that all the stories contained in the sagas were fiction. It was only in 1960, when a Norwegian archaeologist named Anne Stine Ingstad discovered the remains of a Norse settlement at L'Anse aux Meadows, that the lives and deeds of Gudrid Far-Traveler and Freydís Eiríksdóttir were supported by historical evidence. The age of the settlement Ingstad—carbon-dated to around the year 1000—and its location closely matched the descriptions of Gudrid and Karlsefni's outpost in Vinland. Among the more than eight hundred objects uncovered at the site, archaeologists found a bone knitting needle, part of a spindle, and evidence of a loom. As spinning and weaving were almost always performed by women in the Viking world, it is all but certain that the settlement at L'Anse aux Meadows was occupied by men *and* women, just as the sagas of Gudrid and Freydís recorded.

Writing of his compatriots who sailed west across the Atlantic to Iceland, Greenland, and Newfoundland, the first explorers from the Old World to set foot upon the New, a Norwegian chronicler was at a loss to explain why anyone would take such risks without a clear idea of the rewards. "What people go to Greenland and why they fare thither through such great perils?" he asked. The only explanation was "man's threefold nature," he concluded: "One motive is fame, another curiosity, and a third is a lust for gain." As history unfolded, this potent motivational brew of fame, curiosity, and lust for gain continued to drive people to set out into the unknown. It also ensured that the stories they told about far-off lands were widely read—though their tales were often greeted with suspicion.

IN 1298, MARCO POLO, the Venetian merchant who had wandered across the world, was stuck in a prison cell in Genoa. The rivalry between Genoa and Venice for control of the trade routes to Asia had boiled over into war. Polo had traveled these trade routes all the way to China and back again. He poured some of the profits he made from his journey into Venice's war effort, outfitting a warship under his personal command, only to be captured in battle. He spent the rest of the conflict as a prisoner of war. As fate would have it, however, he shared his cell with a well-known author of popular romances named Rustichello. To pass the time and set his story straight, Marco dictated the account of his travels to his cellmate. "From the creation of Adam to the present day," Marco insisted in Rustichello's prologue, "no man, whether Pagan, or Saracen, or Christian, or other, of whatever progeny or generation . . . ever saw

or inquired into so many and such great things as Marco Polo." He
knew there would be doubters—there had always been doubters—so
he made it clear to the reader that all the marvels to follow were real:
"For this book will be a truthful one."

His voyage east with his father and his uncle had taken three and
a half years, or so Marco claimed, taking him past the snowcapped
peak of Mt. Ararat in Armenia, where Noah's Ark was said to rest,
through Georgia and Mosul to Baghdad, capital of the Caliphs and
city of scholars. From Baghdad, he traversed once-mighty Persia,
rambling through country "covered with date-palms" and colorful
parrots "unknown to our climate," to the great port of Hormuz,
where the winds were "so intensely hot as to impede respiration."
From Persia, Polo traveled north and east, into skyscraping mountain ranges that took forty days to conquer. "Ascending mountain
after mountain, you . . . arrive at a point of the road, where you
might suppose the surrounding summits to be the highest land in
the world," he insisted.

Marco spoke of fire-worshippers in Persia and gold-rimmed
mountain temples where monks murmured prayers before the
recumbent idol of some serene god unknown to the West. He told
tales about remote kingdoms where the descendants of Alexander
the Great still reigned and vast, haunting deserts where tricks of
the light produced "extraordinary illusions" and the keening wail
of the windblown sand whispered to the traveler. "Marvelous and
almost passing belief," he granted, except for one who had lived
it. He described the great cities of the Silk Road, inaugurated by
Zhang Qian over fourteen centuries earlier, that now linked Asia
and Europe in an umbilicus of trade—the cities of Yarkand, Khotan, and Kashgar, where caravans of camels bore the exotic riches of

the Orient "to all parts of the world"—and the rolling Asian steppes where Genghis Khan had forged his empire. He even claimed to have knelt before Genghis's heir, the mighty Kublai Khan himself, in his summer palace at Shangdu.

Polo described his years of service to Kublai Khan and his first experiences with paper money, so unlike the gold and silver coins used at home, and jet-black rocks burned as fuel. He recalled sprawling cities that made villages of Venice and Rome—the imperial grandeur of the capital Khanbaliq (now Beijing) and the unrivaled glories of the "Celestial city" of "Kin-sai" (Hangzhou). It all seemed like a romance and a fairy tale, even to Polo himself.

The manuscript of Polo's *Travels* circulated widely in the years after his release from prison, and his stories quickly became common knowledge across the continent. They were fine stories, full of excitement and adventure, but few took them at face value as reportage. "Marco of the Millions" became a stock character in Venice's carnival celebrations, a comic figure of grandiosity and bombast. As far away as England, Polo's name became a byword for exaggeration. He was doubted all his life, and as he lay dying in 1324, his friends implored him to confess his falsehoods and admit that his tales of Persia and India, China and Kublai Khan were invented—a bit of fun that had gone on long enough. He remained adamant to his last breath that all these things and so much more had really happened: "I have not told half of what I saw."

For seven centuries and more, most agreed that Polo's *Travels*, the most famous account of exploration in Western history, was a work of fiction, as doubted and dismissed as the account of Gudrid's travels in the Vinland sagas. And yet, even as Rustichello penned Marco Polo's tale, there were those who knew for certain that many of the things he said were true. Those individuals had traveled the same roads that took Polo across the world to Xanadu. They had seen new worlds too.

Rabban Bar Sauma had been at sea for more than a week when the smell of brimstone wafted in on the wind and the sky itself seemed to catch fire. This wine-dark "sea of Italy" was "a terrible sea," the monk reflected. It was like no body of water he had ever seen. He could well believe the sailors' stories that "very many thousands of people" had "perished" beneath its waves. And now, the first land they had seen in days was a mountain belching hellish sulfur smoke "all day long." At night, when sea and sky became one dark sheet, pillars of fire could be seen bursting forth from its peak. "Some people say there is a great serpent there," Sauma wrote, a dragon lurking in its depths. Perhaps the hellish climate was a sign. Perhaps it had been a mistake to have come so far to explore the land of the Franks.

A fire of another kind set Sauma on his journey. He had been born in Khanbaliq (Beijing) in 1220 to a wealthy Uyghur couple. His parents were members of the Christian Nestorian Church of the East that had reached China in the seventh century. The Mongol Yuan dynasty of Sauma's day was tolerant of many faiths—Buddhist, Muslim, Christian, Shamanic—as Marco Polo would later attest. Sauma's parents had high hopes for their son. At twenty, however, "the divine fire was kindled in his heart, and . . . burned up the brambles of sin," Sauma remembered. He decided to become a monk.

By his middle years, Sauma had become a religious teacher of some repute and a prominent figure in the Nestorian Christian community of the Yuan dynasty. And yet, the world he found in the pages of the Bible drew his thoughts to the lands of Christ and his disciples in the West. He longed to walk in the footsteps of the savior and see the shrines of the saints for himself. His precocious student Markos also had visions of Christendom, and together they began to plan a pilgrimage. "It would be exceedingly helpful to us if we were to leave this region and set out for the West," Sauma told Markos, "for we could then [visit] the tombs of the holy martyrs and Catholic Fathers. . . . And if Christ . . . prolonged our lives, and sustained us by His grace, we could go to Jerusalem." Their friends tried to warn them off, telling the pair that they did not "know how very far off that region is" or "how difficult it will be for you to travel over the roads . . . ye will never reach there." "The kingdom of heaven is within you," they argued; there was no need to seek it in the West. But Sauma and Markos would not be diverted. They "burned to set out on the road," Sauma recorded—as monks, they had already "renounced the world" and were not afraid to die: "We consider ourselves already dead."

Of course, there was precedent for their journey. Chinese ambassadors had reached the borders of Europe before the birth of Christ. In the centuries after, Buddhist monks had regularly crossed the Himalayas to India to visit the birthplace of the Buddha. Two of these monks, Faxian and Xuanzang, had even written down the story of their travels. Sauma would do the same.

Markos and Sauma set off from Yinchuan across the baking Gobi Desert, skirting the treacherous Taklamakan Desert to Khotan, then Kashgar and Khorasan, where they arrived "in a state of exhaustion whereto fear was added." From Khorasan they headed through Mosul to Ani in the Christian kingdom of Georgia, where their path was blocked by war. The road west was too dangerous to continue, but they had no intention of turning back. "We have not come from that country [China] in order to turn back and go again thither," Sauma reasoned, "and we do not intend to endure a repetition of the hardship which we have already suffered. For the man who is tripped up twice by the [same] stone is a fool." They decided to head south for Baghdad, the capital of the Mongol Ilkhanate of Persia, a substate of the Great Khan of China.

When they arrived in Baghdad, they were summoned to the court of the Ilkhan Arghun, the Mongol governor of Persia, who asked why they had come and "what their native country was." They explained that they had come all the way from China in hopes of visiting the Christian Holy Land. With their hopes of reaching Jerusalem dashed, they asked to be allowed to settle in Baghdad among the thriving Christian community protected by the Mongols. Once granted permission, they remained in Baghdad for several years, where Sauma reprised his role as a teacher and Markos rose to become patriarch of the Church of the East. Perhaps they even noticed a trio of Venetian merchants passing through on the same road they had taken west.

SAUMA WAS IN HIS late sixties when the Ilkhan summoned him again in 1287. The Ilkhan wanted to add Syria and Palestine to his domain and realized that an alliance with "the western kings, who are Christians" was the best way to defeat his rival in the region, the Muslim Mamluk Sultanate of Cairo. Markos, now a man of influence at court, knew that Sauma still dreamed of going west and suggested that his old teacher could play the role of diplomat and help forge the Ilkhan's alliance with Western leaders. Despite his years, Sauma was eager for the opportunity to see the lands of Christendom, telling Arghun, "I desire this embassy greatly, and I long to go."

Sauma took a crowded ship across the Black Sea to Constanti-nople, where he was greeted at the gates "with pomp and honour" as a representative of the powerful Mongol Empire and taken to an audience with the Byzantine emperor Andronicus II Palaeolo-gus. In Constantinople, he had at last entered the lands of the Bible. He marveled at the relics of John the Baptist, Lazarus, and Mary Magdalene held in shrines among the marble pillars in the Hagia Sophia. The church's cavernous dome was, he wrote, "impossible to describe . . . to one who hath not seen it."

From Byzantium, he sailed south through the Bosporus into the Mediterranean, the "sea of Italy," with its mountains of fire. In June 1287, "after two months of toil, weariness, and exhaustion," Sau-ma's ship skirted Sicily—and the erupting volcano of Mt. Etna, the sulfur-belching mountain he described in his memoirs—and made landfall at Naples, where he was ushered to see King Charles II. "How art thou after the workings of the sea and the fatigue of the road?" the king inquired. Sauma deftly replied that "with the sight of the Christian king fatigue hath vanished and exhaustion hath departed, for I was exceedingly anxious to see your kingdom."

From Naples, Sauma rode overland through Italy to "Great Rome" only days too late for his audience with Pope Honorius IV. The pope had died while Sauma was still on the road, so Sauma met with the conclave of cardinals instead. They asked all the usual questions—"what is thy quarter of the world, and why has thou come?"—but they also asked more pointed, more suspicious ques-tions designed to test his claim to be a Christian: "Where doth the Catholics live" in the East? "Which of the Apostles taught the Gospel in thy quarter of the world?" "What is thy confession of faith? To what 'way' art thou attached? Is it that which [the Pope] holdeth to-day or some other one?" "How dost thou believe? Recite thy belief, article by article," adding with feigned incredulity that "it is a marvelous thing that thou who art a Christian . . . ha[ve] come upon an embassy from the king of the Mongols." Sauma was surprised by the third degree the cardinals gave him and responded that he had "come from remote countries neither to discuss, nor instruct in matters of the Faith," but to seek the blessing of the pope, visit shrines and relics, and "make known the words" of the Ilkhan of Persia.

While the cardinals debated the successor to the papal throne, Sauma saw the sights. He found St. Peter's as majestic as the Hagia Sophia and toured countless shrines before making his way north to Genoa, which he learned, to his fascination, had "no king, but the people thereof set up to rule over it some great man with whom they are pleased." From Genoa, he continued on through Lombardy and crossed the alpine passes to Paris, where he visited the court of King Philip the Fair. King Philip asked the familiar questions: "Why hast thou come? And who sent thee?" The king's questions were only natural; Sauma was the first person from China to visit France. Sauma explained that he had come for "the matter of Jerusalem," that the Mongols offered an alliance to wrest the holy city from the grasp of the "Arabs."

King Philip was thrilled by the prospect of recovering the city his ancestors had conquered in the name of the cross some two hundred years before and then lost for good in 1244. In recompense, he enabled Sauma to see "everything" exotic Paris had to offer: the "great church" of St. Denis, with its "funerary coffins of dead kings" and its five hundred monks praying "continually" for the souls of the dead; the "30,000" scholars at the university—the envy of all

Europe. The king even showed him the crown of thorns and piece of the true cross brought to France during the Crusades.

Sauma's final stop in Europe was Bordeaux, where he met Philip's rival for control of France, Edward I, the king of England, and again asked to see "whatever churches and shrines there are in this country, so that when we go back to the Children of the East, we may give them descriptions of them." Edward was happy to grant his request. On his return trip through Europe, Sauma finally met the pope, the newly elected Nicholas IV. He spent the holy season of Lent and Easter in Rome, then returned to Baghdad bearing gifts and letters for the Ilkhan of Persia, who was awaiting his return. But Sauma carried back more than an alliance: he brought with him the memory of all the wonders of the new world he had seen.

Rabban Bar Sauma's tales, unlike Marco Polo's, were believed in both the West and the East. In China, his story was inscribed by his fellow monks in the annals of the great monks of the Church of the East. He had returned accompanied by Western envoys who could corroborate his stories: The king of France had dispatched an envoy to Persia with Sauma, and the pope sent a Franciscan friar named Giovanni da Montecorvino on a separate mission all the way to the great Khan's court in Beijing, where he would establish the first Catholic church in China and write an account of the Orient that, unlike Polo's, would be considered true.

Montecorvino's plaintive letters to his superiors back in Rome were practical, even mundane, focusing on the day-to-day struggles of a Catholic mission, with few wonders to enliven his account. Where Polo's *Travels* seemed fanciful because they were so full of wonder, Montecorvino's lack of enchantment or excitement made his account seem accurate, despite its very real limitations and biases.

Many European missionaries would follow Montecorvino to China. Yet it was Polo's tale, doubted though it was, that inspired the next generations of explorers. Among them was a fellow Italian named Christopher Columbus, who made notes in the margins of his well-thumbed copy of the *Travels* and dreamed of new routes to the riches of the "East" that Marco Polo had led him to imagine.

CHAPTER 2

NEW WORLDS

———

I T IS DIFFICULT for us to remember that travel and exploration once took place only on foot and by horse- or muleback; the oceans, above all, remained nearly impassable. But water can connect as well as separate. As the technology of sailing ships improved in the fifteenth and sixteenth centuries, long-distance travel became easier and faster and the world began to shrink. Humans from across the world began to embark on voyages across the open seas, ushering in a new era of discovery, an age of convergence, the age of new worlds.

THE AGE OF CONVERGENCE began with a fleet of more than three hundred enormous "treasure ships" on the Indian Ocean in 1405. Between that year and 1433, the Yongle Emperor, the third ruler of Ming China, launched seven expeditions that would eventually sail to India, Arabia, and Africa—the most extensive maritime voyages in world history to that point. After centuries of rule by the Mongol Yuan dynasty, the Ming, ethnic Han Chinese, were eager to reassert what they saw as Han China's historic place on the world stage, to reforge maritime trade links that had withered in the intervening years, and remind the rulers of Asia where power, wealth, and culture lay. The voyages were meant to impress foreign peoples with the power and sophistication of China and inculcate cultural affinity and economic attachment; they were consciously colossal. The fleets consisted of hundreds of ships, including dozens of 400-foot-long, nine-masted, three-decked "treasure ships." In their holds, the flotilla carried silks and porcelain, literary texts and educational materials, and every sort of trade good that might appeal to the peoples of India or Persia. Commanding the nearly twenty-eight thousand sailors, soldiers, state officials, translators, scholars, doctors, herbalists, engineers, artists, and merchants that made up the expedition was the Muslim admiral Zheng He.

Among the admiral's many advisers and translators was Ma Huan, a Chinese Muslim man from Shaoxing who left a humane and fair-minded account of the three voyages he undertook with Zheng He. In his travels from China to Vietnam, through Indonesia to Sri Lanka, India, Iran, Arabia, and Malindi, in what is now Kenya, Ma Huan and his colleagues collected vast amounts of information, artifacts, and live animals relating to the world they called the "Western Ocean." At every port of call, they peppered locals with questions about geography, religion, social customs, political systems, trade goods, and anything and everything that sparked their curiosity. They drew up maps of new territories, sketched people and costumes and monuments, and collected medicinal plants, works of art, religious texts, and exotic animals—zebras, leopards, ostriches, and giraffes—which caused a sensation when they were displayed upon their return to China.

Arriving at Calicut (modern Kozhikode) on the southwest

coast of India—a generation before the Portuguese navigator Vasco da Gama would become the first European to reach Asia by sea—Ma Huan felt he had at last arrived in "the great country of the Western Ocean," a new world far different from the heavily Chinese-influenced countries of East and Southeast Asia. The center of a vibrant spice trade, Calicut had been a meeting place for merchants from across the world since ancient times, where Greek and Roman merchants could haggle with traders from East Africa, Arabia, Persia, India, and Southeast Asia. Ma Huan was swept away by the startling diversity of the place. "Foreign ships from every place come here," he marveled, to trade for pepper, pearls, and precious stones. There were Hindus, Muslims, Buddhists, Jews, Zoroastrians, and Christians, all with their own rituals and traditions. Ma Huan recorded veneration of "the elephant and ox," a shimmering brass Buddha, and the story of "a holy man named Mou-hsien" [Moses] and his younger brother "Sa-mo-li" [Samaritan] who together "established a religious cult" that splintered between adherents of each brother, whose followers still "hoped anxiously for his [the holy man's] return . . . right down to the present day." Ma Huan was open to new knowledge and fascinated by everything that was novel or strange, and his writing bore no hint of condescension or superiority. The people of Calicut were, he wrote, "very honest and trustworthy. Their appearance is smart, fine, and distinguished." Though the music he heard in India was entirely beyond his experience, he insisted that it was well "worth hearing."

Ma Huan's ability to absorb everything he encountered with genuine curiosity continued when the fleet reached Jeddah, on the coast of Arabia. As a Muslim and an Arabic speaker, he was dispatched to the holy cities of Mecca and Medina as the expedition's official envoy. In Mecca, he joined the throngs of pilgrims from the far reaches of the Muslim world around the Kaaba, one of Islam's most significant mosques, and ensured that an accurate diagram of the "Heavenly Hall" was sketched. In Medina, he paid his respects at the tomb of Muhammad. He found the people "stalwart and fine-looking," even though their complexion seemed to be "a very dark purple" to his eyes. While European visitors often painted Arabs as violent and superstitious, Ma Huan described them in a more sympathetic light. "The customs of the people are pacific and admirable," he recorded. "They observe all the precepts of their religion, and the law-breakers are few. It is in truth a most happy country."

Ma Huan's ethnography and information gathering was not merely for his own entertainment. It was meant both to smooth the way for China's effort to extend its influence throughout the region around the Indian Ocean and to communicate a new image of China to the outside world. After a period of anti-Muslim policy, the Ming dynasty was attempting to pivot toward a less hostile, more cosmopolitan approach to foreign relations. So, while Ma Huan and his colleagues collected information, and Chinese merchants bought up trade goods, the fleets also gave out Chinese literary and educational texts designed to inculcate positive feelings toward Chinese civilization and draw China and the world closer together through shared culture. To ensure that the message of connection and goodwill lasted, the expeditions also raised stone stellae in various landing places to convey China's revived outward-looking worldview. As Ma Huan testifies, in Calicut, Zheng He ordered a stella erected under a grand pavilion where it could be seen by all. Inscribed on the side was China's new inclusive message to the world: "Though the journey from this country [India] to the Central Country [China] is more than a thousand *li*, yet the people are very similar, happy and prosperous with identical customs. We have engraved a stone, a perpetual declaration for ten thousand years."

The stella at Calicut represents one current of the new age of convergence, the side defined by a spirit of curiosity and a genuine desire for connection and exchange. But there were darker forces driving convergence too, the desire for conquest, gain, and domination. The currents were often inseparable. Greed and wonder could coexist; discovery and loss could go hand in hand. Together they would bring millions to the distant shore of some new world and in the process bind the globe more tightly, and irreversibly, than ever before.

THE SIGHT OF LAND was a relief after endless days at sea. The Taíno were experienced seafarers, familiar with the wind and waves. They were born in the center of the Caribbean, made their homes on its islands and their livelihoods upon it. There was nothing unusual about an ocean journey, whether for fish or trade or diplomacy. Water lay at the center of their cosmos and their understanding of their place in the world. But this new voyage, in the cramped hold of a creaking caravel, where neither light nor air could penetrate, had been something they could not have fathomed. Their canoes were open to the sun and sky; their journeys were measured in hours or days. These meager living quarters where they now languished cheek by jowl, week after week, were "so closed in, dark, and evil-smelling that they seemed to be more like burial vaults or charnel houses" than spaces designed to house the living, like "the caves of Hell" itself, according to a traveler who survived a later journey. The nauseous monotony of pitch and roll was broken only by the skitter

of "flights of cockroaches," the scratching of rats, and the pungent
vomit of seasick travelers pressed too close for comfort.

The mind unraveled. There was no relief. "Everything grows
steadily worse," a contemporary wrote of the trans-Atlantic crossing, "the ship labors more and more and the food"—already strange
for the voyagers—"gets scantier and nastier every day." The sea had
always played a central role in Taíno lives and culture, but the vast-
ness of the ocean was inconceivable to anyone who had not experienced it. By the time they glimpsed land, the rank humidity of the
overcrowded hold had given way to a biting cold unlike anything
they had ever felt before. They were far from home indeed.

The Taíno voyagers disembarked on the strange shore with more
than a little trepidation. Still, they were lucky, compared with several of their fellow passengers who were too ill to escape the coffin
of the ship, even when they landed. The Taíno on shore knew that
they were the first of their people to set foot in the new world called
España, indeed, the first people from their hemisphere to cross the
boundless sea. They were strangers here. They did not speak the local
tongue, though they managed to communicate with signs and gestures, a universal human language. Their only guide was the cacique
(chief) of the foreign fleet that had first appeared off their islands the
year before, the man who called himself Columbus. He was already
gaining a reputation for ruthlessness and bad faith. His thirst for
gold was obvious to everyone he met, and this combined with his
habit of kidnapping men, women, and children to serve as interpreters and go-betweens made him impossible to trust. But here in this
new world they had little choice but to follow his lead.

Several of the voyagers had been taken to Spain against their
will. Columbus had seized five Lucayan Taíno men from the

Bahamas, where his ships first landed in October 1492. These Taíno men had ventured out in their canoes to investigate the strange vessels and were abducted. A second group of mostly women and children had been kidnapped from a nearby house. Twenty more Taíno were captured in Cuba and conscripted as interpreters. Their choice to stay or go had been stolen from them, as it would be from many more like them in the years to come. Not all of those who started the journey survived to reach the New World.

The party from Marién, a chiefdom on the large island the Spanish called Hispaniola, was different from those kidnapped from the Bahamas or Cuba. This Marién party included two relatives of their community's cacique, the powerful Guacanagari. The cacique's relatives were "principal Indians," in the language of Columbus. They came as Guacanagari's ambassadors to the king and queen of Spain, Columbus's superiors. Guacanagari was no fool. He was shocked by the sudden appearance of strange men from across the sea in his community, but swiftly reconciled their existence with his understanding of his role and his people's place in the Caribbean. He realized that their presence would change everything and that the Taíno needed more information to understand who they were dealing with.

Taíno cosmology did not include another continent across the sea, but it did include beliefs that helped them reconcile the arrival of the Spanish with their understanding of the universe. They believed that the mother goddess Atabey had given birth to two children, Yúcahu and Guacar. Yúcahu was the creator spirit (zemi) who had populated the earth with plants and animals and the first humans. Guacar, jealous of his brother's prominence, married Guabancex, the zemi of chaos and storms, and together they became the source of all evil and destruction in the world. It was Guabancex who made the hurricanes that lashed the Caribbean and who sent the Taíno's foes, the Caribs, against them. The arrival of the Spanish could thus be viewed through two possible lenses: they were either agents of Yúcahu, sent to aid the Taíno against their Carib enemies, or they were agents of Guacar and Guabancex, sent to sow destruction. Guacanagari seems to have hoped that the Spanish had been sent by Yúcahu and treated them as friends. There was little use in pretending that Columbus and his men had not appeared or that they would simply go away. Besides, Guacanagari and his fellow Taíno were curious too. They hoped to learn more about the Spaniards' ways, their intentions, and the land from which they came. Coexistence would be impossible without understanding.

Guacanagari had gifted Columbus a finely worked belt and a guaíza mask—a "face of the living" constructed from shells and a potent symbol of authority—as a sign of reciprocity and even granted him permission to construct a small settlement within his lands for the men he would leave behind when he returned to Spain. La Navidad, as the Spanish called it, was the first European settlement in the Americas. Like the amity between the Spanish and the Taíno of Hispaniola, the settlement would not last the year. As part of this diplomatic exchange, Guacanagari's relatives had volunteered to undertake a mission to the king and queen of Spain. "Of their own free will [they] wanted to go to Spain," a later Hispaniola historian recorded, though whether they were motivated by a sense of duty to their cacique and their people or by simple curiosity is unclear.

So, Guacanagari's ambassadors stood in the chill of the Spanish town of Palos de la Frontera in the spring of 1493 and tried to wrap their minds around the new world all around them: the garish, constraining clothes, the enormous beasts of burden, the glowering buildings of brick and stone, and the teeming, staring crowds that returned their own gobsmacked gazes with the same combination of unease and wonder. Like Sauma, they were traveling as diplomats but also to witness and report.

From Palos de la Frontera to Seville and all the way to the royal court in Barcelona, the wonders never ceased. They mounted mules—itself a bewildering experience—and set out across a landscape that seemed almost as boundless as the sea. The land, though, was as various and changeable as the ocean had been immutable. Everything was new and different. Nature seemed to struggle here. The bare and stunted trees were a stark contrast to the lush terrain of the Caribbean. They crossed vast dry plains and wide rivers and skirted jagged mountain peaks. And everywhere they saw evidence of the exploits of the people: rows of crops being sowed, village after village and town after town, and an endless stream of traffic along the road. Barcelona was less of a shock after the grandeur of Seville, but it was still hard to get used to the sheer number of people and their constant stares or the narrow confines of the countless streets.

It was April, and the chill of winter was giving way to the first warmth of spring, when they were presented to the king and queen, Ferdinand of Aragon and Isabella of Castile. Columbus was intent on mesmerizing the monarchs with the riches of the exotic "Indies"—a green parrot, gold jewelry, glistening pearls, and other gifts "no one had seen or heard of in Spain before," including the belt and guaíza mask from Guacanagari. When he was finished with his presentation, Columbus ushered the Taíno travelers before the king and queen.

For Columbus, the people of the Indies were a source of riches, as materially valuable as gold and pearls. He had brought them to

Barcelona both as objects of curiosity and as evidence of an untapped source of labor. He hoped they would both help secure the crown's funding for further expeditions and, as forced and enslaved labor, one day make his fortune. In his letters to the king and queen, he painted them as simple, pliant primitives, easy to conquer and convert, a ready source of slaves. But the Taíno had their own reasons for coming to Spain. They were representatives of their cacique and their people, equals in what they hoped would be an ongoing negotiation. And of course, they were curious.

When the Taíno ambassadors were presented to the king and queen, the monarchs fell to their knees, crying pious tears at the possibility of so many new souls to save. As they wept, a choir began to sing. The Taíno were familiar with ritual weeping, so they were not overly surprised by the foreign caciques' performance. As a gesture of goodwill, they asked to be baptized. It seemed an easy way to win the Spaniards' favor. Ferdinand, Isabella, and their son John stood as godparents and gave them new Christian names that befitted their status as Taíno elites: Fernando de Aragon and Juan de Castillo.

Juan remained in Spain as a member of the royal household. He died a few years later, a thousand miles from home. Fernando returned to the Caribbean with Columbus on his second voyage. He found his home already changed by the encounter with Spain. Disease had taken hold. The "sickness of pustules," as one survivor of an outbreak farther west on the mainland remembered, "brought great desolation; a great many died of it . . . and many just starved to death; starvation reigned, and no one took care of others any longer." Taíno society seemed to be unspooling. La Navidad, a symbol of the Taíno's generous accommodation of the new arrivals, had been razed to the ground in an ongoing war with the Spanish. Columbus's first kidnappings had only been a prelude to ever greater pillaging. Enslavement became common, as thousands were transported to Europe to be sold. Thousands more were forced to work in Spanish plantations and mines in the Caribbean and South America. Those who resisted were raped, murdered, or shipped over the sea to become enslaved labor in mines and plantations across the Americas or enslaved servants in elite households in Europe. War raged between the natives and the colonists. Columbus's vision for the future of their newly connected worlds was trampling Guacanagari's. The Spanish, it seemed to the Taíno, were the agents of Guacar and Guabancex after all.

IN THE YEARS AHEAD, thousands more Taíno would make the voyage to the new world across the sea. Few of them would be given any choice in the matter. In 1495, five hundred people who had resisted the Spanish were sent to Europe to be enslaved. Columbus later sent as many as six thousand more people whom he had personally enslaved. After the "discovery" of the American continent in 1498, the Taíno were joined in Europe by thousands of enslaved Caribs, Wayuu, and Warao peoples from Trinidad, Venezuela, and Colombia. In 1528, after his destruction of the glittering Aztec capital of Tenochtitlan, Spanish conquistador Hernán Cortés returned to Spain with a large number of defeated Nahua nobles, whom he presented to the king and queen as trophies of war, including three sons of the vanquished Aztec emperor Moctezuma and one leader of Tlaxcala, the rivals of the Aztecs who contributed to their downfall. A few, however, came willingly. The first people from Mexico to make the journey were the Totonacs, allies of Cortés in his invasion of the Aztec Empire, who arrived in Seville in 1519 to cement their alliance with Spain.

The voices of these Indigenous explorers have been all but erased from the story of the Columbian exchange and the history of exploration. But the echoes of their journeys persist. "The wind now rises, howling and moaning" begins the *Cantares Mexicanos*, which encodes the folk memory of the many Indigenous voyagers to the new world across the sea. "Thus does the ocean seethe and the ship creaks its way along. . . . We behold the massive waves."

KYOTO WAS ABUZZ IN March 1581. An immense crowd of a thousand or more surged through the ancient capital of Japan's emperors and swarmed around the Nanban-ji, the headquarters of the Jesuit missionaries who had first arrived in Japan in 1549, six years after the first Europeans reached the country. As the crowd churned, it seemed as though the building might collapse at any moment. There were already reports of injuries and even deaths at the building's gates, people trampled and crushed as thousands pushed to get a closer look at the men inside. For Oda Nobunaga—head of the Oda clan, Chancellor of the Realm, and the most powerful warlord in a divided country—word of the tumult was cause for concern. Japan had been riven by endless civil wars for a century as local warlords and feudal daimyos clashed for control. By 1581, Nobunaga had already unified a large portion of Japan under his rule, but rivals remained, and civil war still loomed. In such a time, the disturbance at the Nanban-ji was a genuine threat to Kyoto's fragile stability.

As he learned more about the cause of the commotion, caution gave way to curiosity. The crowds, he was told, had gathered around three men newly arrived from Kyushu. The two Jesuits—the Italian

NEW WORLDS   41

Visitor (inspector) of Missions in the Indies, Alessandro Valignano, and the Portuguese priest and translator Luís Fróis—were still a novelty with their beards and black robes, but many in Kyoto had glimpsed Europeans before. The people of Kyoto had come to see the third man, a sort of man none of them had ever seen before, the first known African visitor in Japanese history.

The young African who arrived in Kyoto to such fanfare in 1581 had likely first met Valignano in Mozambique a few years earlier. The Portuguese had begun to colonize this stretch of the East African coast, and Valignano visited the outpost on his inspection tour of Jesuit missions in Africa, India, and Japan. The pair arrived in Japan in August 1579, where they met Fróis, the foremost European expert on the Japanese language. The African man's reasons for traveling across Asia to Japan are something of a mystery. He may have been enslaved and purchased by or given to Valignano in Mozambique, or he may have been hired as a servant or assistant. His first two years in Japan are equally opaque. He must have been with Valignano and

The arrival of European merchants and missionaries became a common theme in Japanese artwork of the Nanban period in the years after the Portuguese first landed in 1543. Africans often appear in such scenes. (The Metropolitan Museum of Art, New York; Mary Griggs Burke Collection, Gift of the Mary and Jackson Burke Foundation, 2015)

Fróis in Nagasaki, in Kyushu, where European traders and the Jesuits themselves had made their first inroads in Japan. But he only steps into the historical record when the trio arrived in Kyoto in 1581.

Valignano and Fróis had traveled to the capital in the hope of securing Chancellor Nobunaga's permission to continue proselytizing. If they hoped to catch the daimyo's attention, their decision to bring along the African member of their entourage was perfectly calculated. However, the Jesuits seemed shocked by the huge crowds that swamped them from the moment they set foot in the city. At 6 feet 2 inches, the African traveler towered above the Europeans and locals. His stature, combined with the color of his skin, marked him as foreign and made him an immediate source of fascination. The constant attention, the obsession with his body, was no doubt alienating for the African traveler, but it proved impossible to avoid. The travelers were followed by gawking crowds all the way to the Nanban-ji, where they were forced to take shelter. The walls trembled and the ceiling creaked as they cowered in their precarious refuge, and the crowd became so obsessed with seeing the African that they splintered the door and crashed into the Nanban-ji, causing a melee. They were only rescued by the timely arrival of Nobunaga's troops, who cleared the way and presented a summons from the daimyo. Nobunaga wanted to see for himself the man who caused such an uproar in his city.

When the three men arrived for their audience, the Jesuits were an afterthought. Nobunaga's retainer, Ota Gyuichi, commented extensively on the "black bōzu [monk] from the Christian country," only adding as an addendum, "The padres came with him." Nobunaga himself was transfixed by the encounter. Insisting that the African traveler's skin color was artificial, that he must have rubbed his skin with ink, Nobunaga asked him to remove his shirt and scrub his skin to prove that it was natural. When this was done, Nobunaga called for his children and his nephew to come and meet the visitor, an opportunity not to be missed. But his interest went beyond mere gawking. He gave his guest a sword, a stipend, a house, and the Japanese name Yasuke—perhaps a translation of the name Isaac or a reflection of his origins among the Yao people of East Africa—and made him a personal retainer. Nor were these rewards and positions simply a matter of Nobunaga's desire to employ the man as an object of curiosity in his court. He seems to have been genuinely interested in Yasuke as a person with important insights to offer about the wider world. Yasuke spoke some Japanese and talked extensively with Nobunaga, who found their conversations to be an inexhaustible source of knowledge and an interesting contrast to those of the missionaries.

That a ruler known for his brusque manner and disdain for others among the Japanese elite took such a liking to Yasuke was surprising on the surface, but it only anticipated a wider Japanese fascination. Writing a decade later, by which point dozens of other Africans had visited Japan with the Portuguese, the Jesuit Jorge Álvares remarked that the Japanese "like seeing black people, especially Africans, and they will come 15 leagues just to see them and entertain them for three or four days." Africans appear in many paintings and illustrated screens of the period and even on the interior lid of a suzuri-bako, or writing box. Sometimes they are depicted as servants carrying parasols for Europeans. But in other images, they appear wearing fine clothes and swords, symbols of status and authority treasured above all other objects and ornaments in Japanese culture—as with the sword that Nobunaga presented to Yasuke, a sign of both favor and respect.

Over the next year, Yasuke was often by Nobunaga's side as he toured his territories. When Nobunaga was attacked and killed by a rebellious vassal in June 1582, Yasuke led the fierce fighting against the traitor outside the residence of Nobunaga's heir. He was wounded and brought back to the Nanban-ji to be treated.

After 1582, Yasuke disappears from the historical record. But there are hints that he lived on in Japan. At the Battle of Okitanawate in 1584, a Black warrior operated a cannon alongside an Indian gunner from Malabar on a warship of Arima Harunobu, an influential Christian convert of Valignano; Yasuke might well have joined his forces after Nobunaga's death. It was Arima, with two other Christian daimyo, who sent the first Japanese embassy to Europe—the Tenshō embassy—from 1582 to 1590. The age of convergence that brought an African traveler to Japan also brought that Japanese embassy to Lisbon, Madrid, and Rome. In a few short years, Japan would close itself off to outsiders—but not before an African voyager whom the Japanese called Yasuke had made his mark.

BY THE TIME THE Tenshō embassy arrived in Lisbon in 1584, as many as two million Indigenous Americans had discovered Europe. So many Native Americans had firsthand knowledge of Europe that when the wary Pilgrim settlers of the Plymouth Colony made their first formal contact with an Indigenous person on a brisk March day in 1621, they were greeted with the words "Welcome Englishmen!" and a request for beer. A few days later, the Abenaki sachem, or paramount chief, whom the Pilgrims knew as Samoset, returned to the fledgling settlement. He was accompanied by a Patuxet companion named Tisquantum who spoke English with even greater fluency. Over time, they learned that Tisquantum (Squanto to the

Pilgrims) had been one of twenty Patuxet and seven Nauset people abducted from Massachusetts Bay in 1614 by John Smith's second in command, Thomas Hunt, who hoped to sell the captives alongside his catch of cod at Málaga, in Spain. Tisquantum was ransomed by Spanish friars who were opposed to the enslavement of Indigenous Americans and made his way to England, where he lived with the merchant John Slaney in Cornhill (in London).

During his stay in London, Tisquantum may well have met another Indigenous traveler from North America, Matoaka, the daughter of the great chief of the Powhatan people, better known to history as Pocahontas. Matoaka had been captured by English settlers of the Jamestown Colony in Virginia during the First Anglo-Powhatan War, which she eventually helped to end. In June 1616, she landed at Plymouth, on the south coast of England, with her English husband John Rolfe and eleven other Powhatan diplomats, before traveling to London by coach. Though she was certainly not the first Native American to walk the streets of London—the Croatan leaders Manteo and Wanchese had arrived with the return of the first of the Roanoke Colony expeditions in 1584—Matoaka's romantic story and status as a "princess" made her a sensation. She met King James at the Palace of Whitehall (though he was so unimpressive that she had to be told later that she had met the king), was entertained by the Bishop of London, and attended a masque organized by the famous playwright Ben Jonson. After several months living at Rolfe's family homes in Brentford, outside London, and Heacham, in Norfolk, Matoaka and her husband sailed down the Thames on the first leg of their return voyage to Virginia. She never made it to the sea. Perilously ill, she was taken off the ship at Gravesend, in Kent, where she died at the age of twenty-one in 1617. She was buried in St. George's Church in Gravesend, though the exact location of her grave has been lost.

TWENTY-FIVE MILES UP THE Thames from Gravesend, just south of Woolwich in the churchyard of St. John's in the sleepy town of Eltham, lies the empty grave of another young Indigenous explorer who never made the journey home. All that remains is a timeworn headstone inscribed "In memory of Yemmerrawanyea a Native of New South Wales who died the 18th of May 1794 in the 19th year of his age." Alongside his mentor Bennelong, Yemmerrawanne was one of two members of the Eora people who arrived in England in 1793, the first Indigenous Australians to discover Europe.

Yemmerrawanne was just sixteen years old when he was first introduced to the British settlers of Port Jackson, Australia, by Bennelong, the primary interlocutor between the British and the Eora. In 1788, the British had sent its "First Fleet" of convicts to establish a British penal colony near what is now Sydney. Bennelong was one of several Eora men and women kidnapped by the British to serve as interpreters, informants, and go-betweens. Unlike many others, he eventually managed to escape and thereafter forged a more equitable working relationship with the British. Though many Eora kept their distance from the British, especially after they realized that these new arrivals often brought violence, kidnapping, and disease, Bennelong's strategic example showed Yemmerrawanne the benefits of knowledge about the foreign invaders. Bennelong had learned the customs and language of the English arrivals in his time working for them and used his familiarity with their technology and customs to improve his standing among the Eora. On one memorable occasion, Bennelong toasted the king of England with British officers while his people looked on warily, then, with a calm calculated to impress the Eora, received a shave. For an impressionable young man like Yemmerrawanne, Bennelong's ability to navigate the strange customs of another world made him a man to follow. When Bennelong decided to join Governor Phillip on his journey back to England in 1792, Yemmerrawanne joined him.

Indeed, there is no evidence that Bennelong and Yemmerrawanne were forced to accompany Arthur Phillip to England: the pair seem to have joined the expedition of their own volition. They had heard much about Britain in the years since 1788 and wanted to see the distant land for themselves, despite the "united distress . . . and dismal lamentations" of their people when they departed. Their pioneering voyage took them from Port Jackson across the Indian Ocean to the Cape of Good Hope, then across the South Atlantic to Rio de Janeiro and north to Falmouth, where they landed on a fair May day in 1793.

In London they were given lodgings in the fashionable West End and outfitted with expensive European clothes of wool and silk before touring the city's most famous sites: the Tower of London, St. Paul's Cathedral, plays at Covent Garden and Sadler's Wells, and the trial of the former governor-general of British India, Warren Hastings, in Westminster Hall. They were even taken to James Parkinson's museum, where they encountered artifacts from the Pacific expeditions of Captain Cook, who had made contact with the Eora twenty-three years before. What they made of the heads of two Polynesian men displayed in the museum is unrecorded.

They enjoyed the novel sights and sounds of London, but never got used to the abominable English weather. They felt cold all the time, and as summer gave way to the chill of autumn, Yemmerrawanne fell ill. They moved to the village of Eltham, just south of London, to escape the insalubrious air of the city. Yemmerrawanne was dosed with all the treatments British medicine had to offer—bleeding, emetics, Dr. Fothergill's famous pills—but his condition only worsened. He died in May 1794 and was buried according to a foreign rite in a frigid foreign soil.

Bennelong became homesick and despondent in the months after Yemmerrawanne's death. He visited Yemmerrawanne's grave regularly to mourn and to perform the death rituals that in England he alone knew, but his thoughts were focused on home. When he finally returned to Australia in September 1795, he quickly cast off the clothing and manners of the British. He had seen enough. According to a British observer, he "laid aside, all the ornaments and improvements he had reaped from his travels, and returned as if with increased relish, to all his former . . . savage habits. His clothes were thrown away as burthensome restraints on the freedom of his limbs, and he became again as compleat a New Hollander, as if he had never left his native wilds."

Yet, for all his rejection of European ways, Bennelong maintained links with the British settlers. He moved easily between two worlds, using his information about the Eora and their homeland to gain favor from the British, and using his knowledge of the British to assume leadership of a clan of some one hundred people living along the Parramatta River.

Unlike Bennelong and Yemmerrawanne, most Indigenous explorers had no choice; they traveled against their will as servants or slaves. A few came as representatives, performers, sailors, or traveling curiosities. The violence and exploitation that so often brought them to foreign shores cannot be overlooked. But these Indigenous voyagers retained their curiosity and their capacity for wonder even in captivity. Many were stared at wherever they went, treated as novelties rather than people. But they merely stared back. They looked upon strange civilizations with interest and discernment. They gathered and considered information about new lands and reported their discoveries to their people back home. They, too, were explorers, mapping new worlds. They became experts in a foreign people, using that knowledge for their own ends. The age of convergence belongs to them as much as to Columbus or Cook.

CHAPTER 3

EXCHANGE

———

THE WORLD BECAME smaller in the age of convergence. As global connections strengthened in the seventeenth and eighteenth centuries, different parts of the world came to know more and more about each other. This process of humanity's self-discovery saw the birth of the scientific explorer, adventurers who sought out the unknown to better understand the world. But this enlightened exploration was only possible through an exchange of knowledge between the peoples of the world. Scientific interest in the natural world transcended the boundaries of race and religion that were beginning to harden in the age of exploration.

BY THE TIME Mary Wortley Montagu crossed the frontier into the Ottoman Empire in 1716, European stereotypes about the "Orient" were well and truly fixed. The accounts of previous European travelers to the Muslim world largely agreed: the civilizations of the Middle East were lascivious, despotic, and unchanging, tantalizing and repellent at once. There was much to gawk at in the East—a veritable feast for the senses—but little for an enlightened Westerner to learn.

When Montagu was told that her husband had been appointed as Britain's ambassador to the Ottoman sultan's court in Constantinople, she found out firsthand how deficient European literature on the Muslim world really was. To prepare for her journey abroad, she read every scrap of information she could find about Ottoman history and culture. She quickly realized that the travelers' accounts in circulation, all written by men, shared the same obsessions—the bathhouse, the harem, the veil—and repeated the same secondhand stories of a society built on sensuality and cruelty. Montagu was skeptical that such accounts revealed much of value about the East. So many of the things confidently described by male travelers were, she knew, off-limits to men. There was little chance a male writer had any direct knowledge of gendered spaces like bathhouses and harems, nor any sense of how Muslim women felt about their place in society.

From the moment her journey began, Montagu was determined that her experience of the Middle East and her account of the Muslim world would be different. She would take the perilous overland route through Vienna and Sofia to Constantinople rather than the quicker, more comfortable sea passage that offered little to see beyond wooden walls and endless light on water. She would abandon the salacious myths she knew her correspondents back home would expect and relate only what she saw and experienced for herself. "I won't lie like other travellers," she told her sister, even if their friend insisted with "ridiculous imagination that I have certainly seen an abundance of wonders. . . . I verily believe she expects I should tell her of . . . men whose heads grow below their shoulders," a common trope in medieval tales of exploration.

Montagu's determination to face the world with an open mind resulted in an entirely new account of the Muslim world, one stripped of sensationalism and brimming with sympathy. Her description of a bagnio, or Turkish bath, in Sofia has none of the usual prurience of other travelers' imaginations. Despite sticking out in her stiff European riding dress, which she recognized "certainly appeared very extraordinary to them," she was made to feel welcome by the other women at the bath: "Not one of 'em showed the least surprise or impertinent curiosity, but received me with all obliging civility possible. I know no European court where the ladies would have behaved themselves in so polite a manner to a stranger." There were "none of those disdainful smiles or satiric whispers that never fail in our assemblies when anybody appears that is not dressed exactly in fashion."

While Montagu was unused to such unconscious and conspicuous nudity, she was careful to assert that there was nothing at all lascivious about the baths. "There was not the least wanton smile or immodest gesture among them," she insisted. Instead, she found the baths to be a welcoming space for female sociability every bit as fizzing with ideas and curiosity as the salons of Paris or the coffeehouses of London. "In short," she concluded, "'tis the women's coffee house, where all the news of town is told," a place of community, conversation, and intellectual exchange.

When the women of the Sofia bagnio discovered the rigid whalebone stays that secured Montagu in her dress, it dawned on her that while male travelers depicted women of the Muslim world as creatures bound in a form of domestic or sexual slavery, these women were freer than their English counterparts in many ways. They were taken aback by the stays and "believed I was so locked up in that machine that it was not in my own power to open it, which contrivance they attributed to my husband." Their own all-concealing clothing, which European writers often equated with erasure, she believed offered a type of freedom unknown to most European women, the freedom to move about their world unwatched by staring, judging eyes. "This perpetual masquerade gives them entire liberty of following their inclinations without danger of discovery," Montagu confided to her sister, and "no man dare either touch or follow a woman in the street." It was thus "easy to see they have more liberty than we have."

By the time she reached Constantinople, Montagu had seen enough to condemn "extreme stupidity of all the writers that have given accounts" of Muslim women or the Ottoman world. Instead of obsessing over exaggerated differences, Montagu argued forcefully that "the manners of mankind do not differ so widely as our voyage writers would make us believe. Perhaps it would be more

Lady Mary Wortley Montagu traveled throughout the Ottoman Empire in the early eighteenth century. Like many women explorers, Montagu's sex allowed her access to people and places that were off-limits to male explorers. (Yale Center for British Art, Paul Mellon Collection)

entertaining to add a few surprising customs of my own invention, but nothing seems to be so agreeable as truth."

Montagu's commitment to empiricism and her willingness to meet other cultures on their own terms, to learn from others rather than simply sit in judgment, not only changed her outlook, but saved the lives of millions. With her five-year-old son in her care in Constantinople, Montagu was more attuned to local cures for the various diseases that struck in childhood. Across Europe, smallpox was among the deadliest of these scourges—mortality rates were as high as 35 percent for the more virulent smallpox strain, variola major. In the Ottoman Empire, Montagu noted, smallpox, "so fatal and so general" in Europe, "is here entirely harmless by the invention of ingrafting," also known as variolation. This practice of intentionally infecting healthy patients with the less virulent smallpox strain variola minor to impart lifetime immunity had been pioneered in China in the tenth century. By the seventeenth century, the practice was in regular use throughout the Muslim world from Africa to Persia.

Reports of the treatment had been relayed to the Royal Society of London by 1714, but most Western medical men remained too skeptical of Oriental medicine to seriously evaluate the practice. With an open, empirical mind and access to the "old women who make it their business to perform the operation," Mary was ideally positioned to consider the real merits of variolation and to admit that the medical women of the East just might have something to offer Western science. She attended several variolation sessions where groups of children were inoculated. No men were present. When she was satisfied that the treatment was safe, she convinced a Scottish doctor to perform the procedure on her own young son.

Montagu knew there would be resistance to any "Oriental"

treatment—she did not tell her husband of their son's inoculation until afterward—but was determined to ensure that her country not suffer for its unwillingness to consider foreign practices: "I am patriot enough to take pains to bring this useful invention into fashion in England, and I should not fail to write to some of our doctors very particularly about it if I knew any one of them that I thought had virtue enough to destroy such a considerable branch of their revenue for the good of mankind, but that distemper is too beneficial to them not to expose to all their resentment the hardy wight that should undertake to put an end to it. Perhaps if I live to return I may, however, have courage to war with them."

When an outbreak of smallpox blazed through England in 1721, Montagu, recently returned from the East, established pioneering variolation trials that would be the first step to developing the world's first vaccine and help make smallpox the first and only disease to be fully eradicated by humankind. Though her balanced, empathetic, and widely read account of the Ottoman Empire could never fully displace stubborn stereotypes of the Muslim world, her commitment to exploring the world with an open mind and a willingness to exchange, to teach, *and* to learn through travel provided a powerful counternarrative that would leave the world a far better, far healthier place.

EVERY EXPLORER RELIES ON local knowledge and expertise. Their voyages are impossible without intermediaries, translators, and guides. Every age and every culture has spawned what I'd like to call "enlightened explorers": those who recognize the vital contributions made by other ways of knowing and appreciate that the world has more to offer than land and commodities. Captain James

Cook was one such adventurer, whose journeys not only depended on but also recognized the expertise of local people. The discoveries of these journeys may later have been used by others for imperial ends, but in their own journeys, these explorers consciously and positively embraced the contributions of those whom they encountered. Cook, for instance, relied on previous European expeditions to find his way to Tahiti in 1769; but once in Tahiti, he sought information about the surrounding seas and islands from local experts, not to manipulate or exploit, but in a desire to know. Among the Tahitians he consulted was a remarkable navigator named Tupaia.

Tupaia was born on the neighboring island of Ra'iatea in about 1725 and had been trained as an *ariori* (priest) before being driven from his home by invaders native to Bora Bora around 1763. By the time Samuel Wallis, the first European to set foot on Tahiti, arrived in June 1767, Tupaia had become a leading figure on the island. His intelligence and curiosity were clear to all. He accompanied Wallis as the Englishman made observations of a rare solar eclipse, and the pair became close. Like many Polynesians, Tupaia had a particular interest in astronomy: the stars were waypoints, helping them to navigate their world of islands and oceans.

Tupaia had always been drawn to discovery. He was raised on stories of his ancestors sailing across the broad Pacific to people of the far-flung islands of the South Pacific. He had been taught the wayfinding skills of Polynesian star navigation, how to use the position of the stars and the character of the ocean currents to travel vast distances without the aid of sea charts or printed maps. His polymathic interest in the world around him—plants and animals, weather and the stars—endeared him to those European explorers with similar interests, and he became fast friends with the naturalist

Joseph Banks, who arrived in Tahiti with Captain Cook aboard the HMS *Endeavour* in 1769.

As the *Endeavour* prepared to depart for its journey through the South Pacific in search of Terra Australis Incognita, the hidden continent believed to rest somewhere in the Great South Sea, Tupaia resolved to explore the world for himself. Although few now journeyed as far across the sea as they had in the time of Tupaia's grandfather, he took pride in the fact that he came from an ambitious seafaring people. Tupaia had personally traveled to dozens of islands in the seas around Tahiti, sometimes sailing for weeks at a time with nothing to guide him but the techniques he had learned from his elders. "With these boats they venture themselves out of sight of land," Tupaia informed an impressed Joseph Banks with a proud gesture at a Tahitian outrigger, adding "they undertake voyages of twenty days." He knew the voyage with the English would be long and perilous, and his family was loathe to see him go, yet Tupaia "stood firm . . . in his resolution of accompanying us," Banks recorded. Tupaia hoped to see with his own eyes some of the distant lands he knew from tales passed down for generations and, in Banks's words, "expressed his intention of going with us to England."

Banks immediately recognized the value of Tupaia's knowledge of the uncharted waters the *Endeavour* was about to traverse. "What makes him more than anything desirable is his experience in the navigation of these people and knowledge of the islands in these seas," Banks explained in his journal. "He has told us the names of above seventy, at most of which he has himself been . . . the benefit which will be derived by this ship, as well as any other which may in the future be sent into these seas, will, I think, fully repay me." With the expedition unable to bear the cost of Tupaia's expenses, Banks agreed to pay the navigator's way: "As soon as he had made his mind known, he said he would go ashore and return in the evening, when he would make a signal for a boat to be sent off for him. He took with him a miniature picture of mine to show his friends, and several little things to give them as parting presents." As the *Endeavour*'s sails billowed and his island home began to recede into the sea, Tupaia and Banks "went then to the topmast-head, where we stood a long time waving to the canoes as they went off." Banks's journals make it clear that Tupaia understood both the enormity of his decision to become an explorer and the irresistible draw of the unknown.

Tupaia swiftly won the expedition over with his navigation methods. He had memorized the names and positions of dozens of islands across the vast expanse of the South Seas. He knew the bearing of each island on his mental map, remembered the path of stars and islands to follow to reach each one, and could even calculate the time it took to travel between them. His imagined geography was staggeringly complex: he could visualize the entire Pacific and knew the positions of reefs and harbors—on approach to one island he guided the *Endeavour* through a hidden gap in the surrounding reef—and could relate the names of chiefs and the history, customs, and produce of countless islands, some of which he had visited himself, some of which he only knew from the oral histories of his people.

A talented artist, Tupaia drew an accurate map in August 1769 showing all 130 islands in a 2,000-mile radius of Tahiti and providing names for 74 of them. He even devised a cartographic system to translate his navigational knowledge into the sorts of measurements Cook and his shipmates could understand. For Cook and Banks, the Pacific islands were a blank region on their European maps, but for Tupaia they were a fully realized world. As Banks once reflected,

"We again launched out into the ocean in search of what chance and Tupaia might direct us to." Tupaia directed the *Endeavour* to New Zealand, Australia, and numerous islands in between. He was often first to land on each foreign shore, acting as interpreter between the Europeans and the peoples they encountered. He warned Cook of the dangers of the martial Bora Borans, negotiated with the Maori (who still revere him), and supplied Banks with information about local history, culture, and wildlife.

Tupaia was more than just a guide for other explorers; he, too, was exploring lands he had only ever imagined. He quizzed Banks on British customs. He traversed jungles in search of plant and animal specimens that he examined alongside the expedition's naturalists, and painted watercolors of people and animals he encountered. He discussed comparative religion with priests he met throughout the journey. Like Banks and Cook, he was fascinated and repulsed by tales of cannibalism and disapproving when he found that some islanders seemed to hold women in less esteem than his people did at home in Tahiti.

What he imagined he would find when his journey ended at the islands of Britain is lost to history. He never completed his voyage of discovery, but died of an unknown shipborne disease among the gabled roofs and teeming streets of Batavia, a Dutch colony in Indonesia.

It was left to other Polynesians to discover the new world of Europe. One was Ahutoru, the son of the king of Ra'iatea, who served as the primary intermediary between Tahitians and the French expedition led by Captain Louis Antoine de Bougainville that arrived in 1768. When Bougainville sailed for France later that same year, Ahutoru volunteered to join him, becoming the first

Polynesian to set foot in Europe. He was a sensation in French society and met King Louis XV and the philosopher Denis Diderot. He
died of smallpox in Madagascar on his way home to Tahiti. Another
explorer, Omai, from the Tahitian island of Ra'iatea, arrived in London in 1774 at the age of twenty-three, where he was reunited with
Joseph Banks, who introduced him to the elite of British society. He
chatted with Samuel Johnson, shook the hand of King George III,
and had his portrait painted by Joshua Reynolds. After two years
in England, he returned to Tahiti with Captain Cook's third expedition and built himself an English house. The map of the South
Pacific might have remained a blank for years to come if not for
the imaginations and navigational skills of pathfinders like Tupaia,
Ahutoru, and Omai.

The consequences of the mapping of the South Pacific, however, were grim. In the years to come, Europeans arrived in ever
greater numbers, drawn by the accounts of Bougainville and Cook
and guided by the charts that Tupaia helped to make. Disease, war,
and conquest followed close behind. As Cook himself realized, what
began as shared curiosity and open exchange could quickly turn into
exploitation and conflict: "We introduce among them wants and
perhaps disease which they never before knew, and which only serve
to disturb the happy tranquility which they and their forefathers
enjoyed. If anyone denies the truth of this assertion let him tell me
what the natives of the whole extent of America have gained by the
commerce they have had with Europeans."

But devastation was not the sole legacy of the Polynesian wayfin-
ders. By engaging with European explorers like Cook and by traveling to Europe, they also inspired some of the earliest critiques of
European imperialism. After meeting Ahutoru in Paris, Diderot

was moved to imagine European imperialism from an Indigenous perspective. His admiration for Ahutoru forced him to confront the oppositional mentality that pervaded the European discourse on non-Europeans. He began to empathize, to wonder what Ahutoru and his fellow Polynesians thought of the arrival of Europeans in the South Pacific. In his *Supplement to the Voyage of Bougainville*, he urged his French readers to consider Polynesian feelings:

> An old man is speaking, the father of a large family. When the Europeans first arrived, he ... looked on them with disdain. When they approached him, he turned his back on them and retreated to his hut. But his troubled silence betrayed his thoughts only too well, and inwardly he mourned his native land and the passing of its golden years. Upon Bougainville's departure, as the Tahitians thronged the shore, clinging to his garments and clasping his comrades in their arms, weeping, the old man solemnly stepped forward and said: "Weep, unhappy Tahitians! Weep! Not, though, at the leaving of these cruel, ambitious men, but at their coming. For one day you will see them for who they are. One day they will return, brandishing in one hand that stick of wood [crucifix] which you see attached to this man's belt and, in the other, the blade which hangs from that man's side. They will come to put you in chains and to cut your throats; they will subject you to their every excess and vice. And one day you will serve under them, and you will be as base, corrupted, and as wretched as they."

Diderot's view of imperialism did not win out in the short term. All that he and Cook predicted would come to pass. And yet, because of men like Tupaia and Ahutoru, imperialism coexisted with a powerful undercurrent of anti-colonialism, a more empathetic vision of an interconnected world based on exchange rather than exploitation.

THE SUN WAS ALREADY high when Carlos del Pino first spotted the ship in the shallow channel south of Coche Island, off the northeast coast of Venezuela, in 1799. The vessel's presence in these waters was a mystery. The agile canoes Pino and his companions sailed could flit between the hidden shoals and sandbanks with ease; the great lumbering ship was likely to run aground. As an experienced pilot of one of these canoes, Pino knew this stretch of coast well enough to know that the new arrival was out of place. Much had happened in the centuries since that first Spanish fleet burst into his ancestors' world—violence, conquest, enslavement, disease—enough to make Carlos del Pino wary of any new arrival.

Carlos del Pino knew the stories of Columbus and the Spanish conquest by heart. They had been passed down to him by generations of his Waikerí people, who first greeted Columbus three centuries earlier in 1498. He knew what had followed in Columbus's wake. He still lived in the shadow of the first permanent Spanish settlement in South America, founded as Nuevo Toledo in 1515, now known as Cumaná, Venezuela. His people still remembered Tamanaco, the legendary cacique who led the resistance against the Spanish in the 1570s. The Waikerí spoke Spanish, had Spanish names, and had assimilated into the Spanish world, but their history and memory were suffused with the legacy of first contact. When a strange ship appeared offshore nearly three hundred years later, Pino was on instant alert.

The threat he feared was not Spanish, but British. Ships of any sort were rare in this channel east of Cumaná, and passing Spanish vessels usually kept well north of Coche. To his knowledge, only prowling British ships risked the treacherous passing through the southern channel. But Pino knew stories about these men too, including the corsair Walter Raleigh, his sack of Trinidad, his journey up the Orinoco in search of gold, and his plundering of Margarita and Cumaná. For centuries, English ships had meant war.

Pino weighed his options. He knew his men were tired. They had loaded into two canoes the night before and sailed through the night toward the forests along the Paria Peninsula, where they hoped to acquire timber to sell back home in Cumaná. But this ship was something altogether new, and he decided to investigate. As Pino aimed his canoe at the unknown vessel, he saw the flash of a telescope from the ship's rail and heard a man's shout from atop its mast. They had been spotted. Even so, Pino was determined to press on, until he heard the thundering boom of the ship's cannon. The folk memories of foreign ships bringing death and destruction flooded back. Pino ordered his boat to turn and escape the range of the cannons. Amid the chaos and confusion, the ship finally unfurled its colors—the red cross of St. Iago—and hailed them in Castilian. Pino breathed a little easier. It was a Spanish ship. Despite their bloody history, the Waikerí had made their peace with Spain.

Pino had never set foot on a European ship before, so when he saw his opportunity, he wasted little time climbing aboard. The ship was Spanish, true enough, but its most prominent passengers were a pair of naturalists from France and Prussia. These men introduced themselves as Aimé Bonpland and Alexander von Humboldt and were, he would soon discover, kindred spirits.

In Humboldt, Pino found a companion in curiosity, a man driven by the shared desire to see and know. Humboldt asked Pino a great many questions about plants and animals, geology and history and seemed to take his answers and his expertise seriously. Pino's exact thoughts about this first encounter do not survive, but we can piece together something of his perspective from the notes his new friend scribbled down in his journal. "By fortunate chance," Humboldt recorded, "the first Indian we met on our arrival was the man, whose acquaintance became the most useful to us in the course of our researches. . . . He was . . . of an excellent disposition, sagacious in his observations, and led by an unceasing curiosity to notice the productions of the sea, as well as the plants of the country." Pino would come to play a central, if oft-overlooked, role in the first of Humboldt's famous South American expeditions. "I feel a pleasure in recording . . . the name of Carlos del Pino," Humboldt wrote in acknowledgment of Pino's vital role, "who, during the space of sixteen months, attended us in our course along the coasts, and into the inland country."

Driven by some of the same impulses and interests that had pushed Humboldt to set out from Prussia in search of the unknown, Pino accompanied the explorers for sixteen long months as they hacked their way through the jungles of South America. In the process, Pino transformed from a pilot, guiding outsiders along a coast he knew from long experience, into an explorer in his own right, traveling farther into the interior of the continent than any of his people had before. He would see lands he had only seen in his imagination and encounter animals and peoples he only knew from rumors.

As evening fell, the *Pizzaro* weighed anchor and then, following Pino's instructions, headed west past the rugged peaks of the Isla de

Margarita and the abandoned pearl fishery of New Granada, to the port of Cumaná. Even with Pino's guidance, the captain of the *Pizzaro* did not risk navigating into the port in darkness. He decided to wait for first light. Pino sat up with Humboldt and Bonpland discussing the local wildlife. The European naturalists were riveted, hanging on to his every word. When they failed to understand his name for boa, or jaguar, or electric eel, he simply described their appearance and mimicked their "manners and forms" until a smile and a flash of understanding spread across the Europeans' sunburned faces.

These eminent naturalists, soon to be towering figures in the annals of European history, were seeing a new world, his world, through Pino's eyes. In the process, Pino began to see his own familiar world through the eyes of another. The "verdant coast" with its mountains "half veiled by mist," the banana groves and sixty-foot cacao trees that "towered over the landscape from the banks of the Manzanares River" seen against a clear azure sky, "unsullied by any trace of vapors," the bright plumage of tropical birds darting between flowering plants, the "dazzling light" that spread through the air, "along the whitish hills strewed with cylindrical cactuses, and over the sea ever calm, the shores . . . peopled by [pelicans], egrets, and flamingos," everything that told the naturalists that they were in a new world, took on a different light for Pino as he saw what had always been the everyday from an outsider's perspective.

At last they landed at Cumaná, where three hundred years before, the Spanish first set foot on the American continent. After driving away the first people they met off the coast of Trinidad in July 1498, Columbus's fleet had sailed north around the Paria Peninsula before heading west through the channel between Coche and the Isla de Margarita to a spot near Cumaná in the Gulf of Pearls.

It was, Columbus wrote, "one of the most lovely countries in the world," rich and bountiful and clearly "thickly peopled." Using hand signs and gestures, his men had asked Pino's ancestors about their gold and pearls. Was there more? Where did they come from? They answered these inquires as best they could in the circumstances, miming that the gold came from farther west. But what the locals really wanted was answers to their own questions. Who were the strangers? Where did they come from? What did they want besides gold? As Columbus recognized, "they were mutually anxious to make inquiries respecting each other's countries." Moments of contact were often moments of mutual curiosity and exchange, whatever horrors may come.

Carlos del Pino led his own party of new arrivals into Cumaná in the same spirit of curiosity and exchange that had motivated his ancestors three hundred years before. He was the living embodiment of all that had changed since that day in 1498—a native who spoke only Spanish and lived in the suburb of a Spanish-American city— and yet, like his ancestors, he was eager to speak with outsiders. He took the visitors to his own garden in the Waikerí suburb, where he proudly presented his silk-cotton trees, his cacti, and his guama trees in full flower. He shared what he knew about each and every plant in his garden, lost in conversation until "night suddenly overtook [them]." "We run about like fools," a deliriously excited Humboldt wrote to a friend in Europe about their first days in the New World. Bonpland joked that he would "go mad if the wonders don't stop soon." They had Carlos del Pino to thank.

Over the next days and weeks, Pino told the naturalists about rattlesnakes and vipers, caiman and pink river dolphins, and about his people's painful history with Columbus and the Conquistadors who followed him. He related the story of first contact and pointed out to them the very spot where the Spanish first arrived. "They show with pride to Europeans the point of the Galera," Humboldt recorded, "so called on account of the vessel of Columbus, which anchored there, and the port of Manzanillo, where they first swore to the Whites, in 1498, that friendship, which they have never betrayed, and which has given them, in Court style, the title of *fideles*."

A keen student of geology, Humboldt was particularly interested in Pino's information about recent earthquakes and the stories he relayed about earthquakes in the distant past. The archives at Cumaná preserved no records older than 150 years—its documents were devoured by termites—so Humboldt was forced to rely on the memories of Pino and his people to reconstruct the geological history of the region. They told Humboldt of the great earthquake that formed the Gulf of Cariaco before the arrival of Columbus and the violent "shocks" of 1530, when tidal waves destroyed the small fort at Nueva Toledo. Pino's community recollected events within living memory with greater detail. Humboldt learned of the devastating earthquake of 1766, when the earth opened, releasing sulfurous vapors and leaving the inhabitants encamped in the streets after most of the houses in Cumaná were "overturned." "The ground was in a state of continuous oscillation," they told Humboldt, "the atmosphere seemed to dissolve itself into water. The rivers were swollen by these sudden torrents of rain . . . and the Indians, whose frail huts easily resist the strongest shocks, celebrated . . . with feasting and dances, the destruction of the world, and the approaching epocha of its regeneration." Such observations, Humboldt realized, allowed him to piece together a new understanding of geological processes and methods of construction better suited to local conditions.

While Bonpland and Humboldt explored this new world through Pino's information, Pino sought to learn everything he could about Europe, their homeland across the sea, and its new science. He peered into their microscope and saw the surface of the moon through the expedition's telescope. When they performed the latest experiments with electricity—animating frogs' legs with electrical currents like the great Italian scientist Luigi Galvani—Pino and his companions asked them to repeat the demonstration so that they could fully understand the science. Pino and the Waikerí considered their inquiries to be no less important, no less systematic than the Europeans' experiments.

Exploration was a two-way street, a mutual exchange of information and expertise, as even Humboldt came to understand. Humboldt recognized that the Waikerí and other Indigenous peoples of Venezuela had genuine interest in "the phenomena of the heavens, and various objects of the natural sciences," and he admired their curiosity, which was "far from being idle or transient" but the product of an "ardent desire of instruction, and discovers itself with an ingenuousness and simplicity, which in Europe are the characteristics only of youth." Humboldt's views were often paternalistic, relegating the Waikerí to the role of inquisitive children rather than recognizing them as equals. What Humboldt failed to see was that both sides in the exchange played the role of teacher *and* student, offering *and* receiving knowledge in turn. When Humboldt asked Pino a stream of excited questions about animals and earthquakes, he became the eager student while Pino became the sage.

The Orinoco was already a legendary river by the time Humboldt began his expedition in February 1800 because of its association with the mythical city of gold, El Dorado. In 1561, the infamous renegade conquistador Lope de Aguirre had crossed the Andes from Peru and sailed down the Amazon in search of El Dorado. He emerged, many murders later, on the Orinoco. Three decades later in 1595, the quest for the golden city continued to draw European explorers to the region, including the notorious English explorer Sir Walter Raleigh, who rowed up the Orinoco on the trail of myths and rumors. Humboldt knew the history of American exploration chapter and verse and was excited to be walking in the footsteps of such legendary figures, even though the treasure he coveted was entirely different. He was not pursuing untold riches or fabled cities, but information about the natural world.

Carlos del Pino, along with Humboldt's mestizo servant José de la Cruz and the Indian translator Zerepe, led the expedition's mules across the llanos and guided its boat through the labyrinth of the Orinoco delta into lands where independent Indigenous tribes still lived free from Europeans. Did they look upon such people and think of their own ancestors long ago before Columbus and Vespucci, Raleigh and Aguirre? Did they envision a different life for their people, imagine what might have been without the Spanish? What is certain is that Pino led the expedition down the Orinoco for reasons closer to Humboldt's than to Raleigh's. He received payment for his expertise, but the records reveal that was not what drove him. Like Humboldt and Bonpland, Pino was fascinated by the natural world and must have hoped to see things no one back home in Cumaná had ever seen before.

The lower reaches of the Orinoco, with its thick groves of palms and mimosa and its night skies glittering with the "innumerable moving lights" of fireflies that seemed "to repeat on earth . . . the spectacle of the starry vault of the heavens," enchanted the Europeans.

Pino, however, only had time for the occasional glance or the hurried answer to an inquiry from Humboldt. His concentration was fixed on wending the boat through the ever-shifting channels of the delta. As the river widened, he was finally able to address the questions asked by his European companions. He pointed out river dolphins, told the Europeans the Indigenous names for the river's many forks and branches, and explained that the firelight they saw in the treetops of the marshy delta were the fires of the Warao people, whose houses were built on stilts to avoid flooding. It was these houses on the water that reminded Amerigo Vespucci of Venice, in his native Italy, and gave Venezuela its modern name.

Humboldt was impressed by the Indigenous knowledge of the natural world. They "discourse continuously" on plants and animals, he later wrote, and "have marked the manners of the crocodile, as the torero has studied the manners of the bull." He had been conditioned to expect simple savages. But the Indigenous people he encountered were contemplative and contributed valuable scientific information.

By the time the expedition reached Angostura in June of 1800, Pino had entered uncharted territory. He could have sailed back to Cumaná from Caracas, his work as pilot done. Instead, he set off on collecting missions deep into the Amazon. They journeyed across the Guiana highlands, investigated the Rio Caroni and the Rio Negro, and confirmed the existence of the Casiquiare channel that linked the Amazon River with the Orinoco. They tracked down the origin story of fabled El Dorado and put to rest the myth of a city of gold in the heart of the jungle. At Lake Valencia, with the help of Pino's friends in Cumaná and the Aragua Valley, who told him about the connection they noticed between the rising temperatures, the dryness of the soil, and the clearing of old-growth forests,

Humboldt formulated the first theory of human-induced climate change. Above all, they packed crate after crate full to bursting with plant specimens and mineral samples for study back in Europe.

After six weeks of trailblazing through the jungle, the expedition returned to Angostura, loaded a team of mules with their vast collections, and headed north across the sprawling savannas of Los Llanos toward Caracas, where Humboldt and Bonpland hoped to find a ship bound for Cuba. When they arrived at Caracas, they found no ships heading for Cuba, so they boarded a small merchant vessel heading for Trinidad by way of Cumaná. When the expedition at last glimpsed the familiar shoreline off Cumaná, they were overcome. "We gazed with interest on the shore," Humboldt reflected, "where we first gathered plants in America," where Columbus first made landfall on the continent. "Among the cactuses that rise in columns twenty feet high appear the Indian huts," the homes of Pino and his people. "Every part of the landscape was familiar to us," Humboldt continued: "the forest of cactus, the scattered huts, and that enormous ceiba, beneath which we loved to bathe at approach of night."

A crowd had already assembled by the time they stepped back onshore at Cumaná. Word had reached the city months ago that the explorers had perished somewhere on the upper reaches of the Orinoco, swallowed by the jungle, never to be seen again. Their reappearance seemed miraculous. "Our friends at Cumaná came out to meet us: men of all castes, whom our frequent herborization had brought into contact with us," and "expressed the greater joy at the sight of us." Perhaps their joy was doubled by the return of a native son? Carlos del Pino was home.

Humboldt and Bonpland did not remain in Cumaná long. The call of parts unknown beckoned them on to Cuba and Mexico,

North America and Peru. In the months and years to come, long after the celebrated explorers were nothing but a memory, did Carlos del Pino continue to regale his family and friends with stories of his voyage? Did his people think of him as an expert on the world beyond and the nature of Europeans? Did he become, in the world of the Waikerí, a famous figure like Alexander von Humboldt? We will never know. But according to Humboldt's account of their travels together, the collections the expedition brought back were "objects of great curiosity" in Cumaná. Once more, two worlds collided, and in the exchange, one of the locals had brought a little piece of the wider world home.

As the Humboldt expedition was drawing to a close, another was being launched to the north—not in the selfless interest of science, but in the political interest of territorial control. In 1800, President Thomas Jefferson dispatched Meriweather Lewis and William Clark of the US Army to lead a "Corps of Discovery" in exploring the 828,000 square miles of land recently purchased by the United States from France.

This expedition, too, relied on Indigenous assistance—but in this case, not given freely. Born in 1800 into the Lemhi Shoshone tribe on the borders of what is now Idaho and Montana, Sacagawea was taken captive by a band of Hidatsa raiders at the age of twelve. At thirteen, the Hidatsa sold her to the French-Canadian trapper Toussaint Charbonneau. In 1804, Charbonneau met Lewis and Clark at Fort Mandan, on the upper reaches of the Missouri River in North Dakota, where the Corps of Discovery was camped for the winter. History—both Sacagawea's and America's—would never be the same.

The acquisition of French territory ushered in an era of westward expansion and manifest destiny that would devastate the world into which Sacagawea had been born. Come spring, Lewis and Clark would continue their journey up the Missouri and over the Rocky Mountains to the Pacific. They used the winter months at Fort Mandan to recruit trappers with experience in the territory and knowledge of the Indigenous languages they would encounter along the way. Charbonneau claimed to speak a number of native languages, but the decisive factor in his selection might have been the capabilities of his teenage wife, Sacagawea, who could speak Hidatsa as well as her native Shoshone. In April 1805, the corps left Fort Mandan and headed northwest with Sacagawea, by then heavily pregnant, helping to guide the way.

Sacagawea proved invaluable to the expedition from the very beginning. In May, she fished the expedition's irreplaceable journals from the waters of a tributary of the Musselshell River in northern Montana when a canoe capsized. In August, she helped negotiate with a Shoshone tribe for horses and guides to take them through the Rocky Mountains. The corps may not have survived the crossing if Sacagawea had not found and gathered camas roots to feed the ailing expedition when their food supplies ran low. When Lewis and Clark sailed down the gorge of the Columbia River and first laid eyes on the endless expanse of the Pacific Ocean, they had Sacagawea to thank.

Sacagawea had navigated and translated for the expedition without any recorded grumbling or complaint. She had traveled some 1,500 miles over many months, had given birth to her son, Jean Baptiste, and endured sickness and danger and the casual violence of her husband, Charbonneau. She had relived the trauma of her kidnapping when the expedition crossed the Missouri River at the very place where she had been taken prisoner four years before. She did all of it with no choice and little say.

But her experience was not all miserable. She was intensely interested in the natural world. She enjoyed telling Clark about the behavior of buffalo and identifying plants unknown to Europeans. And she had been reunited with her nation and her brother Cameahwait in the foothills of the Rockies. As Clark recorded in his journal, Sacagawea "danced for the joyful sight" when a band of Shoshone approached, "and she made signs to me that they were her nation." Even then, she was not given the choice of remaining with her brother. She had to leave her people once again and follow Charbonneau.

On January 5, 1806, Sacagawea finally made her interests known. The corps was in its winter camp at Fort Clatsop near the mouth of the Columbia River when word arrived of a colossal whale on the beach several miles down the coast. Part of the expedition's remit was to catalogue the flora and fauna of the continent, so Clark organized a small party of canoes to investigate. When Sacagawea learned that she was not to be included in the party, she confronted Clark and insisted she be allowed to go. She had heard stories of the sea and though she had journeyed so far westward, she was among the few who had not yet seen it. As Clark recorded, "she observed that she had traveled a long way with us to see the great waters, and that now that monstrous fish was also to be seen, she thought it very hard that she should not be permitted to see either." She wanted to see these wonders for herself, to be able to tell her son someday of all the things they had seen on their long journey across the world. For the first time, she would insist. She would not be left behind.

It took three days to descend the Columbia to the coast and pick their way across the creeks and bays on foot to a steep peak so tall its heights were enveloped in mist. Along the way, they "saw a singular species of fish . . . called a 'Skaite'" that none of them had ever seen before and encountered fourteen Clatsop men and women carrying oozing sheets of blubber. At the top of the sea cliff, the fog began to clear and Sacagawea at last got a good look at the rain-wrapped Pacific. We do not have Sacagawea's words, only Clark's poetic description:

> From this point I beheld the grandest and most pleasing prospects which my eyes ever surveyed, in my front a boundless ocean; to the N and N. E. the coast as far as my sight could be extended, the Seas raging with eminent wave[s] and breaking with great force from the rocks of Cape Disappointment . . . added to the innumerable rocks of eminent size out at a great distance from the shore and against which the seas break with great force gives this coast a most romantic appearance.

When they at last reached the stretch of sand where the whale had been beached, they found the skeleton of a "monster" measuring an incredible 105 feet. Sacagawea had traveled 5,000 miles up rivers and over mountains carrying her young son on her back. She had crossed the lands of her stolen childhood and entered a new world on the coast of the Pacific. She did not choose the journey, but she chose its ending.

THE YOUNG MAN WHO stepped into John Edmonstone's taxidermy shop in 1826 was lost. At sixteen, Charles Darwin felt directionless.

He had come to Edinburgh from England to study medicine, as his illustrious father and grandfather had before him, but he could not muster much enthusiasm for the path that had been chosen for him. All his life, he had been obsessed with the natural world, rambling through the Shropshire countryside collecting beetles and birds' eggs and creating taxonomies of local plants and minerals. In Edinburgh, his medical studies swamped his natural inclinations, leaving him near despair and in need of a lifeline. It was the hope of finding some connection to his childhood interests, some connection to the study of nature, that brought him to 37 Lothian Street and the door of John Edmonstone.

John Edmonstone had been born into slavery on the timber plantation of Charles Edmonstone, on Mirbiri Creek in British Guiana. The jungle that crowded in on the isolated plantation far up the Demerara River was full of fascination for a curious mind like his. Edmonstone's early interest in the natural world around him was channeled in a new direction after a chance encounter with the eccentric Scottish explorer Charles Waterton in 1812. Waterton had come to South America to investigate the source of the poisons used by Indigenous peoples for hunting. His journey took him through the jungles of Suriname and Guiana, where he stumbled out of the woods and into John Edmonstone's life.

By 1812, Waterton knew full well the value of local knowledge. He could be condescending and paternalistic, but he relied on enslaved African guides and porters to navigate through the jungles and on Indigenous experts for information about the plant extract curare, which he would introduce to European medicine. Indigenous knowledge became the basis for a new surgical anesthetic. He also taught several enslaved men, young John Edmonstone among them, the painstaking art of preserving animal specimens, or, as he put it, "the proper way to do birds."

When John Edmonstone was brought to Scotland five years later, he was automatically manumitted under Scottish law. He used his skills in taxidermy to find employment at museums in Glasgow, then Edinburgh. By 1823, he had established his own shop near Edinburgh University on Lothian Street. His skill in the art of taxidermy—a necessity for naturalists and amateur collectors alike—made Edmonstone a well-known figure in academic circles. So when a young Charles Darwin sought some way of finding his bearings in 1826, a kind professor recommended he visit Edmonstone and learn how to preserve birds.

Edmonstone's shop became a lodestone and a refuge for Darwin; his taxidermy lessons reconnected him to his youthful interests in the natural world and inspired him to dream of a different future outside medicine. Edmonstone's stories of his travels with the Waterton expedition and his descriptions of the flora and fauna of South America inspired Darwin to join the celebrated expedition of the HMS *Beagle* in 1831. On that journey, he would find himself stepping into the same worlds Edmonstone had described to him on Lothian Street and preserving zoological specimens for further study—including the famous Galápagos finches that helped form the core of his theory of natural selection—using the skills Edmondstone had taught him.

Thus, the knowledge and inspiration of a formerly enslaved explorer helped to change the course of Darwin's life, and with it, our understanding of life itself.

CHAPTER 4

INTERPRETING

———

THE KNOWLEDGE EXCHANGED by explorers in the eighteenth and early nineteenth centuries allowed the West to construct narratives about civilization that were used to justify imperialism and exploitation. But these narratives were always contested by other groups of often-overlooked explorers, men and women who used their travels to interpret the world and its peoples in altogether different ways.

DEAN MAHOMET WAS NOT the first South Asian to set foot in the British Isles when he landed at Cork in 1784, though it certainly felt like it. Nothing in his twenty-five years had prepared him for the months-long voyage from Calcutta down the Hooghly River to Madras, then across the Indian Ocean to the Cape of Good Hope and north through the Atlantic to St. Helena and Dartmouth. He had no experience with ships or the sea, no point of reference to equip him for week after week of endless, empty vistas. At Madras, he was "led by curiosity" to explore the first of the British East India Company's three presidency towns. During the onward journey to Cape

Colony on the southern tip of Africa, he was delighted by the sight of "several kinds of finny inhabitants of the liquid element" he had never seen before. However, what remained fixed in his memory years later was a storm in the South Atlantic that "burst . . . with resistless impetuosity over our heads, incessantly raging for three days." "The howling of the tempest, the roaring of the sea, the dismal gloom of night, the lightning's forked flash, and the thunder's awful roll," he later wrote, "conspired to make this the most terrifying scene I ever experienced." When the green Irish coast at last broke the monotony of endless blue, relief warred with trepidation. "When I first came to Ireland," Mahomet recalled a decade later, "I found the face of every-thing about me so contrasted to those *striking scenes* in India, which we are wont to survey with a kind of sublime delight."

Mahomet had been fascinated by Europeans since his boyhood days in Patna, the capital of Bihar, one of the three states ruled by the Nawabs of Bengal in northeast India. His father, who died when Mahomet was just a boy, had been a *subedar*, the second-highest rank an Indian officer could achieve in the army of the British East India Company (EIC), one of many Indian and European powers jostling over the remains of the dissolving Mughal Empire. Perhaps it was a longing to feel closer to the "gallant father" he never really knew that drew Mahomet to the British officers in Patna. In any case, he started following them through the city. One day, when Mahomet was eleven, he followed a group of scarlet coats to a soiree at a tennis club, where he met a young Irish officer recently arrived from Cork. Godfrey Baker was in the midst of building up his household in India and asked young Mahomet "how I would like living with the Europeans." Over his mother's objections, Mahomet agreed to join Baker's household, explaining "with eager joy, how happy he could make me, by taking me with him."

For the next fourteen years, Mahomet remained at Captain Baker's side, first as steward of his household, then as an army officer in his own right. Together they crisscrossed the subcontinent as the EIC's entanglements in India thickened and conflicts over the spoils of the Mughal Empire proliferated. From Patna, they marched through Buxar to the banks of the Karamnasa River, then down the Ganges valley through the untamed hill country to the British capital of Calcutta. In Calcutta, Mahomet stepped into a different world, one where the influence of Europeans was written in brick and stone.

From Calcutta, Mahomet and Baker ventured north to Murshidabad, the court of the Nawabs of Bengal and home of Mahomet's ancestors. In 1775, they headed west up the Gangetic plain to the Hindu holy city of Varanasi and on through Lucknow to the decaying Mughal capitals of Allahabad and Delhi. Outside Buxar, India was an alien place for Mahomet. In a place as dizzyingly diverse as India, Mahomet's travels with Baker and the British Army were expeditions into unknown worlds, even for a native son. When Baker was recalled to Calcutta in October 1782, he decided he'd had enough of army life and began making plans to return to Ireland. After more than a decade together, he invited Mahomet to travel to Europe with him, and Mahomet leapt at the opportunity to explore the world. The years of wandering through India had given him a thirst for new horizons. So, "having a desire of seeing that part of the world," Mahomet resigned his commission and, after a last jaunt to Dhaka and the mangrove jungles of the Sundarbans, the pair set sail for Ireland.

DESPITE THE PRESENCE OF his friend and mentor and his interest in Europeans, Mahomet struggled to find his place in Ireland. He "felt some timid inclination" and "consciousness of incapacity" as an outsider in Europe. To speed his assimilation and remedy these feelings of inadequacy, he began refining the English he had picked up from Baker in India and studying English literature. Soon he was both a fluent English speaker and an eloquent writer, with confident command of the European canon and the ability to compose poetry and quote Seneca and Milton. In 1786, he took his assimilation one step further and married Jane Daly, a young woman from the Irish-Protestant gentry that governed Ireland. Through Baker

Determined to counter persistent European misinformation about his native India, Dean Mahomet used the story of his own explorations to present his homeland in a more authentic, more positive light. To manifest his authority, he exchanged his usual European attire for the sort of romanticized Indian costume his audience expected. (Colored lithograph by T. M. Baynes; Wellcome Collection)

and, after Baker's early death, Baker's wealthy brother William, Mahomet found employment, mixed with the elite of Irish society, and was embraced by that society in turn. Still, for all the acceptance he found in Cork, there were nagging signs of disrespect that made him feel like he would never truly belong.

As Europe's engagement with Asia intensified in the eighteenth century, interest in the exotic "Orient" grew. Novels, plays, and travel narratives describing adventures in the "mysterious East" were gobbled up by curious Europeans, who swallowed the stereotypes whole. Time and again, Mahomet was confronted with infuriating assumptions about Muslims and offensive portrayals of Indians that had no relation to reality. In 1788, Voltaire's brutally Islamaphobic *Mahomet, the Imposter: A Tragedy* was staged in Cork. In Voltaire's words, the play had been "written in opposition to the founder of a false and barbarous sect." In 1791, Isaac Bickerstaff's *The Sultan; or a Peep into the Seraglio* treated audiences to a salacious look behind the walls of the harem, a subject of ongoing fascination for Europeans, despite its marginal place in the lives of actual Muslims. Such fantasies proved more popular than the firsthand reporting of travelers like Mary Montagu who had actually seen the inside of a harem.

These works often influenced how travelers viewed India. Henrietta Clive, wife of the British governor of Madras, reached India in the decade after Dean Mahomet's departure. She had made the journey expecting to find the romantic world of the *Arabian Nights* come to life. But the India she found was not the fabled dreamscape of her imagination. The first Indian prince she met at Madras in 1798 was "a hideous little old man much more like an old woman" who possessed nothing of the "Oriental splendor" she expected: "He had neither pearls as large as pigeon's eggs nor diamonds. . . . In short there is nothing like Haroun Alraschid [Harun al-Rashid] or Viccer Giafor [Vizier Jaffar] to my great disappointment." Her visit to a harem proved equally deflating: "I expected it to be like the sera-glios in the *Arabian Nights*, but I am told it is only a number of small rooms not unlike . . . a convent where each lady lives in *one* room. I expected to have heard fountains of marble spouting up rose water and cushions of the finest embroidery. But not at all—the rooms were as dirty and poor as possible." Clive was interested in India, but only as a fantasy. In her preference for the exotic "Orient" over the real India, she was entirely typical.

By 1793, Mahomet had heard enough. As one of the few Indians in Ireland, and one of the only English-literate South Asians in the British Isles, he felt he was well suited, perhaps even obliged, to set the record straight and present Muslims and Indians as they actually were. Rather than penning an op-ed or a pro-Indian polemic, he decided to recount the story of his wanderings through India with Captain Baker. Travel narratives were hugely popular in the eighteenth century, but Mahomet's decision to publish his *Travels* was about more than the appeal of the genre. At the time, Mahomet had thought of his journey through India as an expedition of discovery. With the absence of anything like an Indian national identity and in the face of the subcontinent's stunning cultural, lin-guistic, religious, and ethnic diversity, Mahomet felt as though he were exploring a new world from the moment he stepped beyond Bihar. In Murshidabad, he watched a procession of the Nawab of Bengal, to whom he was distantly related, with rapt attention. Its "glittering appearance" was both a source of pride and a symbol of what India had once been but was no longer. In much of India, he was an outsider.

Living in Europe, however, transformed Mahomet's understanding of India and his travels. From this new perspective, he could see what united Indians rather than divided them. His time in Europe allowed him to construct an identity that transcended the bounds of faith and region and to reframe his travels in a way that presented his homeland to a European public in a new, more positive light.

Mahomet makes his intentions clear from the first page. "The people of India," he begins, "are peculiarly favoured by Providence in the possession of all that can cheer the mind and allure the eye, and tho' the situation of Eden is only traced in the Poet's creative fancy, the traveller beholds with admiration the face of this delightful country, on which he discovers tracts that resemble those so finely drawn by the animated pencil of Milton." From the start, he was translating India into terms that his European audience could understand, demonstrating his familiarity with the European canon, and comparing India to ancient Greece and Rome, cultures Europeans revered. Indians, he continues, are not just blessed with natural bounty, but by "the exercise of benevolence and good-will to each other, devoid of every species of fraud and low cunning."

As he describes his travels through India, he presents each new discovery in a way that subtly undermines the most persistent European stereotypes of India and Indians. Whereas European accounts often portrayed Muslims as licentious, cruel, and fanatical, Mahomet presents Muslims as sober, temperate, and full of empathy. They refrain "from the use of strong liquors," he tells his readers, eat modestly, and have few diseases, leaving the comparison with Europe unsaid but implied. They "meet death with uncommon resignation and fortitude," like models of British stoicism, and yet "use every means to comfort" and console the families of the recently departed. They are "strict adherents to the tenets of their religion" without veering into fanaticism. Far from being licentious, they hold women "so sacred . . . that even the soldier in the rage of slaughter will not only spare but protect them." Even the harem and the dancing girls, twin obsessions of prurient European imagination, are not what they appear to the unenlightened. The harem is simply "a sanctuary against the horrors of wasting war," while dancing girls are refined artists who have "nothing of that gross impudence which characterizes European prostitutes."

But Mahomet was not simply concerned with defending his own faith. His travels to such holy sites as Varanasi brought him closer to Hindus than he'd ever been as a child in Patna. His travels in Europe enabled him to view Indians, Hindu and Muslim alike, through a new lens as Indians. As such, he presents Hindus not as the cunning, servile, superstitious figures of European narratives, but as pious, "ingenious," and honorable. "However strange their doctrine may appear to Europeans," he insists, "yet they are much to be commended for the exercise of the moral virtues they inculcate, namely, temperance, justice, and humanity. . . . Amidst a variety of extravagant customs, strange ceremonies, and prejudices, we may discover the traces of sublime morality, deep philosophy, and refined policy. . . . Hindoos are men of strong natural genius, and are, by no means, unacquainted with literature and science. . . . We may trace the origins of most of the sciences, in their ancient manuscripts. Even before the age of Pythagoras, the Greeks travelled to India for instruction."

European travelers occasionally echoed Mahomet's more positive views of India, especially when, like Eliza Fay, the wife of a young English barrister who hoped to practice law in Calcutta, they brought a new perspective to well-worn stereotypes. Sati, the ritual practice of Hindu widows self-immolating on their husband's funeral pyres, figured prominently in European accounts of the barbarity of India. Indeed, British attempts to end the practice were held up as exemplars of beneficent British rule and used as justification for the West's mostly hollow "civilizing mission." Though shocked by the possibility of the practice, Eliza Fay, who traveled through India at the same time as Mahomet, noted that she had never seen the ritual performed; moreover, she couldn't find a single European who had seen it firsthand. Although part of the colonial machine, her viewpoint nevertheless differed from that of so many of the men who had decried the practice Fay granted that the stories of sati were so commonplace that the practice was more than likely real, but assessed the ritual from the perspective of a woman, reframing it as a consequence of the inequalities between men and women that existed everywhere, even in England. "I am well aware that so much are we the slaves of habit *every where*," she wrote home to her family, "that were it necessary for a woman's reputation to burn herself in England, many a one who has *accepted* a husband merely for the sake of an establishment, who has lived with him without affection . . . would yet mount the funeral pile with all imaginable decency and die with heroic fortitude," just as Hindu women sometimes did. What was invisible to Western men was clear as day to Eliza Fay—a colonialist but also a woman. The lens of the explorer mattered.

Dean Mahomet's perspective provided a more thorough challenge to conventional European narratives. At Allahabad he had marveled at the "sublime air of grandeur" of the ancient palace, which rivaled "the old triumphal arches of the Romans." Calcutta, "that great emporium of wealth and commerce," was the definition of refinement, "where people of rank appear in a style of grandeur far superior to the fashionable éclat displayed in the brilliant circles of Europe," while the mangrove forests known as the Sundarbans were the definition of natural beauty. The winding channels of the mangrove jungle were a "feast" that "delighted [the] eye with a variety of new scenery. . . . The water . . . appeared like an extended mirror reflecting the tall trees that grew upon each border. Creation seemed to be at rest, and no noise disturbed the silence which reigned around, save, now and then, the roaring of wild beasts in the adjacent woods: the scene was truly great, and raised to unaffected grandeur, without the assistance of art."

Dean Mahomet was not the first South Asian to travel to Europe. Nor was he the first person in the British Isles to publish a firsthand account of India. Yet, seeing through European stereotypes to reveal the real India required the eye and pen of an Indian explorer. Dean Mahomet, the first South Asian author in the English language, led the way.

IN SEPTEMBER 1794, just as Dean Mahomet's *Travels* was appearing on the bookshelves in Ireland, a young Scottish surgeon named Mungo Park stepped into the London headquarters of the African Association and offered his services as an explorer. Founded in 1788 and led by the doyen of British exploration, Sir Joseph Banks, the African Association's stated mission was to cast new light on the "Dark Continent." Though Europeans had been trading and enslaving on the African coast for centuries, they knew staggeringly little about its interior. As late as 1800, most Europeans were still relying on ancient Roman sources for their sketchy information about the continent's interior. The African Association hoped to remedy this deficiency in the name of science, commerce, and, most important, abolition.

The overlap between the membership of the African Association and London's increasingly active antislavery societies was considerable and intentional. For many of its most prominent members, exploration could be reimagined as another tool in the fight against slavery. British antislavery was largely a movement of moral suasion. Abolitionists hoped to convince the public of the evils of slavery and the slave trade and put public pressure on Parliament to change its laws. To illustrate the brutality of enslavement, those who had experienced it published harrowing accounts. Ships' surgeons told of the horrors of the Middle Passage, and activists toured the country displaying whips and chains and other instruments of torture.

Firsthand information from explorers about African civilization provided yet more ammunition for the antislavery campaign. Ignorance about African society had allowed slavery's apologists to present Africans as unfeeling, unthinking savages, natural slaves who were better off in bondage, encouraging the wider white populace to fool itself into believing that the enslavement of Africans was benign. The African Association realized that the only way to explode these pernicious stereotypes was to travel to the continent's interior and gather evidence of how Africans lived outside of slavery: to recognize them as full human beings.

By the time Mungo Park offered his services in 1794, the African Association's attempts to chart the Niger River and locate Timbuktu, the lost city of Mansa Musa, had resulted in two men dead and one expedition abandoned before it began—only reinforcing European ideas of Africa as a dangerous, unknowable land of violence. When Park began his ascent up the Gambia River in June

1795, many assumed he would never be seen again. His reappearance two years later was therefore greeted with astonishment. His survival transformed him into a celebrity overnight, ensuring that his account of his adventures—*Travels in the Interior of Africa*—was an immediate sensation. When he died in mysterious circumstances on a second expedition to the Niger in 1806, he became a legend of African exploration.

Mungo Park represented a swashbuckling, heroic icon of the explorer that would capture the imagination of generations—the image of a man who braved untold dangers and journeyed into uncharted lands in quest of pure knowledge. Like all explorers, Park's motives were in fact far more mixed—fame and fortune certainly played their part—but he helped to construct a lasting archetype. And though his account of capture and escape, suffering and peril certainly excited public interest, the information he relayed did something more: it opened up previously unknown worlds for his readers. And in the process, he helped his readers reimagine Africa and Africans.

In Park's narrative, Africa is not merely a backdrop for death-defying feats. Nor were Africans presented as stock characters or props. Just as Dean Mahomet reinterpreted Indians as three-dimensional people worthy of respect, Park presented Africans not as stereotypes, but as full people. Within weeks of setting out from the mouth of the Gambia River for Senegal guided by Johnson, a local man who had once been enslaved in Jamaica and spoke both English and the local languages, and Tami, a blacksmith traveling home to his native country in the interior, Park and his comrades were on the brink of starvation. Their provisions had run out. The trade goods they carried to exchange for food and smooth their way were mostly gone. The small quantity of cash they carried had been seized by a local ruler as a tax on travelers passing through his domain. The situation was so dire that they were reduced to chewing on straw to "combat hunger for the day."

As evening fell, a woman passed balancing a basket on her head. She noticed the dejected travelers and divined their predicament. As Park recorded, "she asked me If I had got my dinner." When she heard their tale of woe, "the good old woman, with a look of unaffected benevolence, immediately took the basket from her head . . . [and] presented me with a few handfuls [of groundnuts] and walked away, before I had time to thank her." Park was overcome. The woman had not questioned his story or his character. She had simply "listened to the dictates of her own heart" and helped a stranger without a moment's hesitation. Park reasoned that, like most people, she had probably known hunger. The experience of "her own distresses made her commiserate those of others." It was a lesson in empathy that Park would never forget, a real-life illustration of the powerful abolitionist slogan of universal human brotherhood: "Am I not a man and a brother?" The result of Park's experiences in Africa was a simple yet forceful message: "Whatever difference there is between the Negro and the European, in the conformation of the nose, and the colour of the skin, there is none in the genuine sympathies and characteristic feeling of our common nature."

He even turned the well-worn cannibalism trope on its head. Since the concocted medieval travel narrative of John Mandeville through the age of Columbus and Magellan, European explorers had used rumors of cannibalism to delineate European "civilization" from non-European "barbarism." Labeling Indigenous Americans, Africans, and Polynesians with this ultimate taboo was a handy way of denying their full humanity and justifying conquest. Park's account of the African perspective made clear who the barbarians really were. The ones with the unsatiable hunger for human flesh were European enslavers. "They were all very inquisitive, but they viewed me at first with looks of horror, and repeatedly asked if my countrymen were cannibals," Park wrote of an encounter with the Mandika people of Mali. Such a perspective forced Europeans to reckon with their own history.

In 1853, David Dorr stood in the swirling sands that whispered over the plain, lost in thought, oblivious to all around him. The heat, the wind, the cameleers guiding tourists from Cairo to Giza, Dorr noticed none of it. His gaze was fixed some 470 feet above, where the pinnacle of the Great Pyramid of Khufu scraped the sky. This was the moment he had been waiting for all his life. He had traveled for three years and thousands of miles to reach this very spot in Egypt. He had crossed oceans and scaled mountains, navigated teeming cities and traversed sea and desert to look upon the fabled works of Djoser and Khafre, Ramesses and Khufu with his own two eyes. He was, he wrote, "awe struck" by the immensity of the pyramids, but even more so by what they represented. They were, he believed, evidence of his own humanity inscribed in stone. He was a pilgrim in search of his origins and his ancestors, of evidence that Africans like him had a place in the pantheon of "great civilizations," that he and his people were the equal of those who claimed descent from Greece and Rome, men who claimed to own them. Standing in the shadow cast by the Great Pyramid, the proof seemed undeniable.

Dorr's quest had begun with a promise of freedom. The son of a white father and an enslaved mother, Dorr had been born into

slavery in New Orleans in 1827. In 1851, however, his master offered
him manumission in return for acting as his servant on an extended
tour of Europe and the Holy Land. Dorr leapt at the opportunity
both to escape the stifling confines of American slavery and to return
home a free man. As he contemplated his journey in his writings,
however, Dorr felt internally divided. In Europe, he would find the
history and culture of his enslavers, but it was his culture and his
inheritance too. Well educated and widely read, he could already
imagine how it would feel to stand in the footsteps of Shakespeare
and Byron, to tread the same earth as Napoleon and Wellington,
and to glimpse the landscapes celebrated by Constable and Turner.
And he knew how rare it was for an enslaved American to walk such
hallowed ground. He was excited to experience all that Europe had
to offer. In his heart, however, he was drawn to the lands of the Bible
farther east.

From New Orleans, Dorr and his master crossed the Atlantic to
England, where he felt that for the first time in his life, he breathed
the air of freedom. It was not simply the fact that he was treated as
a man rather than a slave, but also the explorer's thrill of entering a
different world. As the fugitive slave William Wells Brown put it in
1855, "the gray stone piers and docks, the dark look of the magnif-
icent warehouses, the substantial appearance of everything around,
causes one to think himself in a new world instead of the old."

Dorr found the English welcoming and remote in equal
measure—"it would puzzle the double-wide intellect of a hermit to
tell what one was thinking"—but what struck him more forcefully
than all the industry and wealth was the realization that the British
had once been consigned to the fringes of civilization and were now
at its center. The British, he reflected, "were wearing the skins of the

beasts of their forests in the days of the Caesars' invasion." They were
the barbarians. "Now," he reasoned, "they are the most civilized and
Christian power on this earth." It augured well, he thought. There
was hope yet, as he saw it, for his own people, despite their chains.

In France, he wandered among the ruins of the first castle he had
ever seen and stood rooted in reverence in the nave of Notre Dame,
"that venerable old monument of reality and romance. I approached
it like a timid child being baited with a shining sixpence. As my feet
touched the sill, a peal came from the belfry, one of those sonorous
twangs, that have made so many hearts flinch for hundreds of years
in the 'Bloody Bastille,' and it vibrated from my timid heart to all
parts of my frame. At this moment a reverend father offered me his
hand . . . and he led me quietly into that vast 'sepulchre of kings'."

As his eyes adjusted to the gloom, French history seemed to
materialize around him: the glow of stained glass, the glimmer
of bronze plaques and marble monuments, and the subtle signs of
everyday people, the footsteps of generations of pilgrims and parish-
ioners worn into the very stone. The "departed worth" surrounding him was so overwhelming that Dorr reflexively bowed his head
"with a submissive heart," as if unable to look such grandeur in the
eye. As he did so, he realized he was standing on the grave of a king
and jumped back, only to find himself standing on the memorial slab
of a queen. He had to laugh. Here he was, a slave in American eyes,
trampling royalty under his feet.

From the enchantment of Paris, Dorr headed south and east
through Lyon and Aix to Byron's Geneva, then through the Alps
to Germany before returning to Paris for the winter of 1851–52 via
Brussels, Ghent, and Waterloo. He spent Carnival, the lively festival
preceding the fasting of Lent, in Rome, where he stood with a crowd

of ten thousand under the vast vaults of St. Peter's to catch a glimpse of Pope Pius IX. Further south, the bay of Naples was as beguiling as he expected, but he found the city itself disheveled and its citizens jittery and morose. Perhaps living in the shadow of Vesuvius among the frozen remnants of Pompeii and Herculaneum trained them to expect the worst at any moment, he reflected.

Traveling east, "where the wise men lived," Dorr encountered a world in which the Bible seemed to come alive. On the rocky coast of Anatolia, the lone surviving wall of an ancient church in Smyrna "resounded back the voice of St. John," who had first preached from this very spot the Epistles Dorr heard every Sunday. This merging of the familiar and the exotic heightened as Dorr's ship sailed through the Bosporus Strait to Constantinople. A shout from the captain brought Dorr excitedly to the rail. Shimmering in the distance he saw "an immense number of steeples, towers and minarets; to the eye no city on earth need look prettier. It was, indeed, the fairest sight I ever beheld." However, of all the marvels Constantinople offered, none was as surprising or as gratifying as the sight of a Black man dressed in Turkish clothes. To Dorr's delight, this man who moved about the city at the center of an enchanted crowd, with a white woman on his arm, who looked the sultan himself in the eye and shook his hand, was a freedman from Tennessee. His name was Frank Parish, and he radiated confidence and command. He knew his worth. He bowed to no one. For a Black American like David Dorr, it was a sight to behold.

From Athens, Dorr continued up the Adriatic to Venice, then on through Verona, Florence, and Genoa before heading back to Paris for the winter. In the spring of 1853, he set out across the Mediterranean for Alexandria and Egypt. For more than two years he had soaked up the wonders of the Western world. He visited Homer's birthplace, the spas at Baden, and the reputed home of Shakespeare's Juliet. But when it came time to tell the story of his voyage, he always began in Egypt.

Dorr would later describe his primary motivation for his journey as the desire to look "with his own eyes and reason at the ruins of the ancestors of which he [was] the posterity"—not because no one had seen the pyramids before, but because few Black Americans of his day could ever hope to. It took the "eyes and reason" of a Black American to reconstruct and reinterpret ancient Egypt in a way that was meaningful to Black people back home. Like his more celebrated contemporaries David Livingstone and Richard Francis Burton in Africa and Arabia, Dorr was exploring territory unknown to *his* people and reporting back what he found. The insights and impressions of Dorr's white companions almost never appear in his narrative. Their perspective is irrelevant. It is David Dorr's story, and that story is an African American one.

On the plains of Giza, Dorr constructed an alternate genealogy of civilization, one that centered on Africa and Africans. "Greece and Italy," the seedbeds of European civilization, "were schooled in all that they excelled"; but it was here, in Egypt, he argued, "that Moses obtained his fundamental rules of governing nations . . . for he was 'learned in all the learning of the Egyptians.'" The wonders of Egypt represented for Dorr "a living language of their scientific majesty," the unsurpassed monuments evidence of genius and a source of pride and ambition. The Egyptians, Dorr believed, were first and foremost Africans, his people, and the ancestors of so many millions held in bondage. "Ask Homer," he declared, "if their lips were not thick, their hair curly, their feet flat and their skin black."

———

AT THEIR CORE, EXPLORERS are interpreters. They not only discover, but also explain and interpret distant lands and peoples for their countrymen. They shape how the rest of us view the world and understand their place within it. Dorr's narrative—published in 1858, forgotten, and rediscovered in the late 1990s—functions in the same way as the many slave narratives published in the years before the Civil War. These harrowing accounts of enslavement, suffering, and escape were purposely designed to interpret a foreign land—Southern plantations—for sympathetic readers in Europe, Canada, and the Northern states of America. In these narratives, readers were confronted by men and women who thought and felt as they did, undermining pernicious stereotypes of Africans. In this respect, David Dorr had two publics he was traveling and writing for. For white America, he was offering proof of the sophistication of Africans, both in his playful, yet scholarly prose and his descriptions of ancient African civilization.

For Black America, enslaved and free, he offered pride and hope. His writings conveyed pride in a past that was every bit as glorious as the European pasts of Greece and Rome, and hope that someday their people might ascend to lofty heights again. After all, they had done it before. Dorr had seen the proof for himself on the plains of Giza. Now those who read his story could see it too.

CHAPTER 5

GUIDING

———

THE CENTURY BETWEEN 1850 and 1950 saw the apogee of Western imperialism and the golden age of the media coverage of the heroic Western explorer. This was the age when George Mallory gave voice to the motivations of a generation of explorers by explaining his desire to summit Mt. Everest simply "because it's there." But in the shadows of such celebrated adventurers were thousands of guides, translators, and porters of every race and creed. Like the famous figures they worked with, their motives for exploration were not purely idealistic. But in carefully reading the records, what emerges is a picture of men and women who shared the same sense of adventure, spirit of inquiry, and boundless curiosity as Mallory. The expeditions could not have taken place without them, but in the tales of the Western explorers, they were usually nameless. Like the mountains, they were simply "there."

HENRY STANLEY HAD no idea how to organize an expedition. He had proposed to find the Scottish missionary-explorer David Livingstone with all the confidence that ignorance affords.

Livingstone had become a household name in the English-speaking world after publication of his best-selling *Missionary Travels* in 1857. He was an icon of Victorian exploration who combined death-defying bravery with a burning commitment to stamp out the last embers of the slave trade in Africa. Livingstone was the paternalistic "Civilizing Mission" personified, a man who sought to bring Christianity and British culture to those he considered less fortunate. His disappearance somewhere in the heart of East Africa in the 1860s only made him more famous, inspiring Stanley's ambition to ride Livingstone's coattails to renown.

With the *New York Herald* sponsoring his African expedition, Stanley set off for Zanzibar in 1871 to prepare. He pored over every account of African exploration he could find, especially those of Sir Richard Francis Burton, John Hanning Speke, and James Augustus Grant, who between them had been the first recorded Westerners to find the sources of the Nile, the holy grail of African exploration. Stanley began his own expedition in Zanzibar because Burton, Speke, Grant, and Livingstone himself had done the same. From their accounts, Stanley learned that his expedition would require a significant amount of local labor: soldiers for defense, guides, and porters to carry supplies and trade goods needed to smooth their way. In all, he estimated he would need more than a hundred men.

Still, the practical details of organization eluded Stanley. "I was totally ignorant of the interior," he confessed in his account of the expedition, "and it was difficult at first to know what I needed . . . it would have been a godsend, I thought, had either of these three gentlemen, Captains Burton, Speke, or Grant, given some information on these points; had they devoted a chapter upon, 'How to get ready an Expedition for Central Africa.'" Without a guidebook, Stanley's first step was to seek the advice of a local fixer, Sheikh Hashid. Hashid knew everyone in Zanzibar and told Stanley exactly what supplies he would need—which type of cloth or color of beads each people along the way would accept—where to buy them, and who to hire as guides and porters. He also informed Stanley that he was in luck: several of Burton and Speke's "Faithfuls" still lived in Zanzibar. Indeed, the famous waYao guide, Sidi Mubarak Bombay, was only a short distance away on Pemba, the northern island of the Zanzibar archipelago. Hashid knew him well, had heard the excitement in his voice when he recounted his journey to discover the sources of the Nile, and assured Stanley that he would "jump with joy at the prospect of another expedition."

Before long, Stanley had recruited the core of his expedition. Bombay was as eager to join him as Hashid had promised. He told an awestruck Stanley, who had read about Bombay's exploits in Burton's and Speke's narratives, that he was "ready to do whatever I told him, go wherever I liked." In return, Stanley made Bombay the leader of the guides and porters and provided him with a wage, a rifle, and a new uniform befitting his position. Still, Bombay was driven by more than monetary gain. The five other "Faithfuls" who signed on for another expedition—Ambari, Ulimengo, Baruti, Uledi, and Burton's former valet Mabruki—had similarly mixed motives. The pay Stanley offered was certainly attractive, though many would have considered it poor recompense for the risks they undertook. They were propelled by other motivations that European writers too often fail to recognize in the Indigenous members of expeditions: curiosity, adventure, fame. While that part of the Western world that idolized the intrepid white explorers might never resound with the name Ambari or Mabruki, their travels made them celebrated figures in their own communities.

All six "Faithfuls" still proudly possessed the medallions they had received from the Royal Geographical Society for their role, as the inscription read, in the "Discovery of the Sources of the Nile." Not one of them had hocked their prize for cash or pawned the proof of their exploits to make ends meet. It would have been understandable if they had. These were medals granted by a foreign body they had never visited, inscribed in a language they did not know. And they were made of precious metals to boot. If money had been all that mattered to the "Faithfuls," the medals would have been sold off long ago. But instead, their owners kept them, proof of who they were and all that they had seen and done.

This desire for reinvention was something that Stanley understood completely. He was the bastard son of a teenage mother who abandoned him and a father he had never known. He grew up in a workhouse in Wales and was still masquerading as an American to hide the embarrassing reality of his birth. He had come to Africa to prove his worth and erase his past, to make his adopted name his own.

AFTER MONTHS OF SEARCHING and a 700-mile trek through the jungles and savannas of East Africa on the trail of rumors and secondhand reports, Stanley and his expedition at last located Livingstone at Ujiji, on the banks of Lake Tanganyika in modern Tanzania, on November 10, 1871. In later accounts crafted for the press, Stanley claimed to have greeted Livingstone with the words, "Dr. Livingstone, I presume?" "Yes," Livingstone was said to have replied, "and I feel thankful that I am here to welcome you."

The reality of their fateful meeting, however, was quite different from the story Stanley later told audiences back home in America and Britain. His famous greeting is absent from both men's journals, only appearing in newspaper stories long after their initial meeting. Likewise, it was not Livingstone who welcomed Stanley to Ujiji. In fact, the evidence shows that Stanley was met by a Shupanga guide named Abdullah Susi and a Yao translator named James Chuma and that Stanley, who had rehearsed his meeting with Livingstone to ensure it would read well in the press, was more than a little startled to be greeted in English by an African with the words, "Good morning, sir."

"Who the mischief are you?" Stanley sputtered.

"I," came the assured response, "am Susi."

Stanley was at a loss. He had expected to meet David Livingstone, the long-lost Scottish explorer, in the African bush. He had never dreamed that he would encounter a pair of African explorers who had already gone farther and accomplished more than he could imagine.

Chuma and Susi had been exploring with Livingstone for almost a decade by the time they reached the village of Ujiji. Susi had originally signed on as a woodcutter on the expedition's steamship on Livingstone's Second Zambezi Expedition in 1863. Chuma had been with Livingstone ever since Livingstone freed him from slavery at the age of eleven in 1861. Together, they explored the Zambezi and Lake Nyassa and traveled to Zanzibar and Bombay, where Susi worked as a dockhand and Chuma studied at Wilson College until Livingstone returned from Britain in 1865 to launch an expedition in search of the source of the Nile. Their reasons for exploring were complicated. Chuma, for one, refused to believe that his family had sold him into slavery when he was two years old, and continued searching for his relatives. But when other porters, guides, and servants returned home, Chuma and Susi always stayed with Livingstone and eagerly signed on for expedition after expedition.

When Livingstone died in Zambia two years after the fateful meeting with Stanley, Chuma and Susi, together with another of Livingstone's African guides, Jacob Wainwright, buried Livingstone's heart in the shade of a mpundu tree and carved a memorial to the explorer in its bark. Then, with dozens of other African members of the expedition, they wrapped his remains in a bark shroud and carried it more than a thousand miles through the bush to the coast at Bagamoyo, ignoring the plea from another white explorer they encountered to bury him where he lay. They had carried him in life, when he became too sick to walk, and they would carry him in death, back to his home, where his family could mourn him and his body finally find rest in Westminster Abbey.

On that final journey, Chuma, Susi, and Wainwright met Livingstone's friends and relatives in Scotland, visited a workhouse and an agricultural show in England, and were honored with medals at the Royal Geographical Society in London for "duties strenuously performed." They shaped Livingstone's legacy by helping to edit his journals for publication, offering details on geography and peoples and drawing whole river systems from memory. In the introduction to *The Last Journals of David Livingstone*, editor Horace Waller acknowledged the trio's vital contribution: "Their knowledge of the countries they traveled in is most remarkable. . . . I found them actual geographers of no mean attainments."

Both men returned to Africa and joined further expeditions, Susi with Stanley's Congo Expedition of 1879–82 and Chuma with

Joseph Thompson. Thompson recognized what few then knew and most have now forgotten: that African men and women like Chuma and Susi "in their own special way" had "done so much to open up Africa to science and communication." The exploration of Africa was as much an African achievement as it was a Western ambition.

The common image of the explorer is of a man alone in the wilderness, boldly blazing new paths into the unknown. This picture of self-reliance is fantasy. Explorers relied on local knowledge and local muscle: guides to point the way and teams of porters to carry equipment and supplies. Neither guides nor porters are usually included in histories of exploration. Guides are usually dismissed as locals leading "real" explorers through lands they themselves already know. But guides often traveled into lands about which they knew little better than the Europeans they guided. Porters are usually presented, if

James Chuma and Abdullah Susi were two of the thousands of Africans, Asians, Polynesians, and Indigenous Americans who led the expeditions usually credited with mapping the globe. Chuma and Susi guided the Scottish explorer David Livingstone on the voyages through Equatorial Africa that made him famous. (Well/BOT/Alamy Stock Photo)

they're presented at all, as drudges, beasts of burden no different from an expedition's pack animals, backs bent, necks bowed under the weight of their loads. This is certainly how many explorers saw porters, all but erasing them from their accounts and denying them status as explorers in their own right. But porters' eyes were not always fixed on the ground beneath them, on the loads they carried, on the work to be done, on the next weary step.

Even when they are acknowledged in the accounts of Western explorers, guides and porters are usually presented as driven by money and need rather than by more noble ends. We need to scratch beneath the surface as we read the accounts of Western explorers to discover that local guides and porters were as motivated by curiosity and wonder and imagination as their employers, as prone to both excitement and exhaustion. Only then can we see them, finally, as explorers.

The only difference between these shadow figures of the official narratives—a Mubarak Bombay or an Abdullah Susi—and Stanley or Livingstone is that their voices have been largely silenced. But glimpses of their curiosity and determination remain. Sometimes they even left records in their own words, inscribed with their wonder and joy for all the world to see.

BY 1923, Ghulam Rassul Galwan had reached heights that he had only ever dreamed of. As Aksakal of Ladakh, he was the chief native assistant to the British joint commissioner based in Leh and the most influential liaison between the British government and the various Pathans, Baltis, Kashmiris, Shina, and Changpa, who made their homes on the high plateau nestled between the fearsome Karakoram range and the soaring Himalayas at the headwaters of the river

Indus. His prominent position made him one of the elites of Leh, but his friends and neighbors were drawn to him as much for his inviting nature and charm as for his official prominence. At forty-five, his movements were graceful and his bearing still elegant despite his years of arduous labor. He spoke almost every language to be found in this polyglot corner of the world—and acquired many more from far beyond the borders of Ladakh. He had an eye for beauty and an ear for music, was a gifted musician and a sought-after storyteller. Though some doubted that all the adventures he recounted were true, his most far-fetched stories were the most popular. In the flickering firelight of a winter's night, when the snow fell and the wind howled, Rassul was asked again and again to tell the tale of his journeys across the world with men from England, America, and Italy. He was always happy to oblige. These were his favorite stories, too, because they held the key to his unlikely rise to his elite position.

Rassul's travels were an inseparable part of his identity. In Leh, he was the man who had trekked across barren deserts and over towering mountain passes, the man with friends on three continents, the man who, because of his travels, had the ear of the British commissioner. He first began to write down his story in 1901, when he served as caravan bashi for the expedition of the American explorers Robert and Katherine Barrett. With the Barretts' help, he honed his English by reading the King James Bible and a seventeenth-century travelogue during the many "periods of mere waiting, without adventure or work," that punctuated an expedition. At only twenty-three, he already "wanted very much to write a book." Tales told around the fire were ephemeral. But books were forever. Books had fascinated him since childhood, when he first beheld the colorful vellum texts treasured by the lamas in their mountain monasteries. In their crackling pages, they seemed to hold the secrets of all ages, an unbreakable inheritance to be passed down from one generation to the next. If he could only write his own book of his own adventures, his name and his deeds might live on, like the Buddhist scriptures.

For fourteen years Rassul sent page after page of "the story of my happened," as he described it, to Robert and Katherine Barrett, who helped him compile and edit the thin sheets of his manuscript into a singular memoir of a caravan bashi of the Himalayas, with Rassul's own language left intact: a true record of the voice of the man with whom they had been writing back and forth for over a decade. The resulting book is a rare account of exploration from the perspective of one of the many unseen men and women who led the way for more celebrated Western explorers. For Ghulam Rassul Galwan and countless other guides, porters, and interpreters like him across the globe, exploration was their calling and their profession, as central to their sense of self as it was to Merriweather Lewis or Henry Morton Stanley.

FOR A YOUNG BOY of the Ladakh valley on the western edge of the Tibetan Plateau, the world beyond the cold embrace of the mountains beckoned. Leh was a caravan town on the road between India in the south and western China to the north. In the summer, when the snow melted in the passes, merchants crowded in from far and wide, bringing whispers of the outside world. For young Rassul, Leh's tree-lined bazaar seemed to hold clues to all the mysteries of the world. Here he heard a babel of foreign tongues and saw wares from distant places he only knew from stories. He was swept away by all of it and dreamed of nothing else but foreign lands.

When a British official was posted to Leh, Rassul rushed to see the family of white people for himself. He found everything about these outlanders fascinating—theirs looks, their clothes, their language, their furniture—and after studying them for hours, built replicas of it all out of tin and paper, using white adobe to recreate the skin color of the Europeans. Though a Muslim himself, Rassul marveled at the vibrant frescoes painted on the walls of his local Buddhist temple and copied the scenes on flat stones and the walls of Leh's mudbrick fort. He pored over the pages of any book he could get his hands on and imagined himself living in the worlds contained in their pages. He wasn't interested in other children's place-bound games and preferred to play alone, dreaming "that [I] went long way in the world."

By twelve, Rassul was desperate to go to school, but the fees were too high for his mother to afford. "It is rich men's work, reading and writing," she told a crestfallen Rassul, "not ours." She had been abandoned by her father and her husband in turn—both had gone north to live in Yarkand—and was raising Rassul and his three siblings on the money she scraped together as a "winnow-woman." What she needed was for Rassul to pull his weight. "All time you do different than other boys," she sighed, "other young boys make good work." She sent him to live with a tailor to earn his keep and learn something of a stable trade, but his new master was cruel and Rassul was restless—the stationary work of a tailor held no appeal for a daydreamer—so he ran away. He longed to roam wherever his imagination took him. "I was hurry for be old," he later wrote. "And in head all time in night made rich, made meet with big men . . . and saw many different countries. . . . All the time I played in head with this matter." Poor boys in Leh could dream about adventures in distant lands too.

Eventually, Rassul's mother relented and allowed her irrepressible son to find work more suited to his active imagination and his thirst for the exotic. In his early teens, he worked as a servant for a Kashmiri merchant who sometimes paid his mother to winnow grain. Though he started out mostly fetching wood and hauling water, his job with the merchant opened new horizons for Rassul. He brought supplies of grain to the Indian soldiers who manned the local fort and brought food and fuel to encampments of Europeans traveling through to Kashmir or Yarkand. Always a quick study, he learned Kashmiri from the merchant and Hindustani from the sepoys. Rassul's work for the Kashmiri merchant even offered him the chance to join the expedition of a European anthropologist.

Dr. Trall was traveling through Leh on his way south to Kashmir as part of a project to measure the "face, feet and heads" of everyone he met. The journey would only take two months to complete, but it was still farther than Rassul had ever been before. He had wandered throughout Ladakh on trips to gather firewood and had climbed into the foothills of every side of the valley, but the other side of the mountains remained a mystery. When the expedition reached a place called Feyangtakpo (modern Phyang), it hit him all at once that "beyond that place I had not been." He was only 18 miles from Leh and yet it felt like he had traveled halfway across the world. He asked his more experienced companions how long it would take them to reach Kashmir, thinking it could not possibly be much farther. They laughed at his naivete. Their journey had only just begun. Still, for Rassul, Feyangtakpo "seemed to me very far."

The trip to Kashmir was one that many people in Leh had made before. Even so, it transformed Rassul's life. He welcomed the first real money he had ever earned. Most of all, he was enraptured by new horizons; two months of exploration would never be enough.

The moment he set foot back in Leh, Rassul searched for another expedition, and, against his mother's wishes, sought a position with the famous caravan bashi Mohammad Isa. Isa had been leading European expeditions into Central Asia and the Himalayas for years and had a well-earned reputation as a peerless guide and mountaineer. Rassul reasoned that working for Isa as a porter would give him the best chance of seeing more of the world.

In 1890, Isa was preparing for a journey north through the Karakoram Pass to Yarkand and on around the edge of the deadly Taklamakan Desert to the fabled Silk Road outpost Kashgar. The caravan would carry six British envoys and officials, including George Macartney, incoming consul-general at Kashgar, and the celebrated Captain Francis Younghusband, who had already made a name for himself as an explorer in the Changbai Mountains of Manchuria and for his overland trek west across the breadth of China through the Taklamakan to Kashgar, then south through the uncharted and nearly unpassable Mustagh Pass to the Pamir Mountains and the Hindu Kush in India. The region north of Ladakh was a void on British maps and a potential flashpoint in the competition with Russia for control of Central Asia. Younghusband had been dispatched with a band of Gurkha soldiers to chart the road between Leh and Yarkand and clear the region of the troublesome Hunza raiders who preyed on its caravan traffic.

Rassul begged Isa to include him in the expedition, even offering to work without pay. Isa, however, thought Rassul, in his early teens, was too young for the journey and insisted he stay behind in Leh. As a last resort, Rassul appealed to Younghusband directly. Though he spoke not a word of English, Rassul's enthusiasm transcended language. Younghusband was taken with the young Pathan and agreed to hire him as a porter for the expedition.

Younghusband recognized himself in Rassul. He, too, had caught the exploration bug at an early age and made his first expedition through China in his early twenties. He had not asked for permission from the British Army to make the journey that had made him famous. He knew exactly how it felt to need to see the world. In his twenties, Younghusband had been inspired by stories of his uncle Robert Shaw, who had journeyed to the fabled city of Kashgar in Central Asia some thirty years before. Some five years after Shaw's death, Younghusband tracked down his uncle's house in Dharamsala, and as he gingerly made his way inside, he was overcome. Everywhere he looked were the crumbling remains of maps and manuscripts. "I was among the relics of an explorer," he later wrote, "at the very house in which he had planned his explorations, and from which he had started to accomplish them. I pored over the books and maps, and talked for hours with the old servants, till the spirit of exploration gradually entered my soul." He was hooked.

For Roy Chapman Andrews, who grew up in Wisconsin reading the accounts of the great nineteenth-century explorers—Younghusband and Sven Hedin, Henry Morton Stanley and Fridtjof Nansen—"there never was any decision to make. I couldn't do anything else and be happy . . . the desire to see new places, to discover new facts—the curiosity of life has always been a restless driving force in me." He felt born to be an explorer: "Always there has been an adventure just around the corner—and the world is still full of corners."

This motivating curiosity was certainly true of Rassul, as it was of many non-Western explorers, including scores who risked their lives to map the Himalayas. The British employed a number of Indian "pundits" to perform many of the most difficult and dangerous mapping missions in the borderlands between Russia, China, and British India. They reasoned that an Indian disguised as a merchant or a pilgrim—with surveying equipment secreted in trade goods and trigonometrical charts hidden in prayer wheels—stood a better chance of completing their work unnoticed than a European. The pundits were trained in surveying and spycraft and dispatched on expeditions that sometimes took years and often cost them their lives. Their recompense for braving such dangers was too small to attract fortune hunters or the desperate. Those who chose to become pundits were driven by something other than money.

Kishen Singh, part of a remarkable family of pundits from Uttarakhand, was recognized with a gold watch inscribed by the Royal Geographical Society in London. His cousin Nain Singh was awarded the Royal Geographical Society's Patron's Medal in 1877 "for his great journey and surveys of Tibet and along the upper Brahmaputra." According to Henry Yule, who accepted the medal in Singh's honor, Singh's "observations have added a larger amount of important knowledge to the map of Asia than those of any other living man." This recognition as an explorer, it turns out, was enough to make all the hardship worth it. As Rudyard Kipling says in *Kim*, referring to a pundit modeled on men like the Singhs, "Do you know what Hurree Babu really wants? He wants to be made a member of the Royal Society by taking ethnographical notes. . . . Curious—his wish to be an FRS [Fellow of the Royal Society]. Very human, too." What surprised Kipling's blinkered character should not surprise us: the impulse to explore is universal.

Many Western travelers found it hard to believe that poor men like Rassul would be willing to do backbreaking work and face constant dangers to guide a Western expedition through the mountains and deserts of the Asian steppe for any reason other than pay, and yet: "The secret is that these men . . . love adventure just as much as their employers," Younghusband insisted.

RASSUL GALWAN'S CURIOSITY was richly rewarded. His journey to Yarkand brought him face-to-face with people and places he could only have imagined. At the village of Panamik, the party got wind of a Russian naturalist in the area on a butterfly collecting expedition. In the midst of an ongoing competition between Britain and Russia for control of Central Asia, Younghusband and Macartney saw every Russian as a potential spy seeking to sway locals to their side, to chart a path for a future invasion of British India. For Rassul, the tensions of the "Great Game" merely made Russians more interesting. "I longed to look him," Rassul later wrote of this first encounter with a Russian, "and see what sort of man is a Russian man. I never had seen a Russian man." When he at last saw the Russian in a garden in Panamik, he saw that the man was just "a white man and poor," hardly the sinister spy of the British imagination. Rassul was more impressed by his encounter with Shukar Ali, the only Ladakhi guide to have braved the perilous Mustagh Pass with Younghusband back in 1887. At Panamik he also met a Chinese interpreter, an Afghan guide, and a Gurkha servant boy who became his "very good friend."

Between Panamik and Yarkand, the caravan road took the party into the heart of the Karakoram range and over the treacherous 18,000-foot-high Karakoram Pass. As the most junior man in the caravan, Rassul was assigned to look after a worn-out pony and quickly fell behind the others. Even though it was 31 miles long, it was important to traverse the Depsang Plain and cross the pass in a single day. There was no waiting for stragglers to catch up. Rassul was forced to climb the steep ascent to the pass on foot and totally alone. He wept in frustration when he realized the pony could go no further, but there was nothing else to do except ascend through the pass.

At more than 17,000 feet, the scale of the Depsang Plain was terrifying at first, "as bare as a gravel-walk to a suburban villa," Younghusband recorded in his account of the journey: "Away behind us the snowy peaks of Saser and Nubra appeared above the horizon like the sails of some huge ships; but before us was nothing but gravel plains and great gravel mounds, terribly desolate and depressing. Across these plains blew blinding squalls of snow, and at night, though it was now the middle of summer, there were several degrees of frost." It was a totally alien landscape, like stepping out onto the surface of the moon. "For a while I was afraid," Rassul confessed, "because I not had seen before such country." Then he saw the tracks of the expedition's horses. There was a path to follow. As he continued down the pass, his terror slowly dissipated, replaced by gratitude and wonder.

After the monotony of the Depsang Plain, Yarkand was a feast for the senses. Yarkand was the last major stop for caravans heading north across the Taklamakan Desert—known far and wide as the desert of no return—and people streamed in from every direction, all of them fascinating to Rassul. It seemed as if the entire world was converging on Yarkand. He wanted to see it all. Above every other novelty, Rassul "longed" to see the Chinese amban (governor) and could hardly stand still when the official's procession wound through the city's narrow streets with red flags flying and the hollow sound of a gong echoing down the earthen alleys. He begged Isa to let him visit Yarkand's bazaar and accompany Younghusband and Macartney to their audience at the amban's palace. He soaked up every sight and sound—the palace's peaked-tile roof, its magnificently painted gate and carved guardian lions—and carefully noted the protocols of a diplomatic meeting. "All that I kept in my head," he wrote with delirious pleasure. He did not dare forget a thing.

In 1892, Rassul's third expedition, in the yak caravan of Lord Dunmore and Major Roche, took him even farther afield, to Kashgar. The first stage of the journey across the Depsang Plain and through the Karakoram Pass was now familiar, but three days out from Yarkand, he remembered why he had traveled. The caravan had been silently trudging across the featureless plain in silence. Everyone was too tired to talk or sing, even Rassul, who normally kept up a steady flow of song or conversation. Then, as evening neared and the sharp light of the Himalayas turned golden, they entered a valley of sublime enchantment. "Both sides were beautiful, high, and steep and grey," Rassul noted. "There were rocks like castles. That seemed us wonderful." Their exhaustion melted away. "We said each other: 'We forget our tired in the looking this wonderful sight.'" That night, they camped in the thick grass under a lone tree—a rare sight at this barren altitude—on the edge of a crystal mountain spring. They ran "and laughed very plenty" despite their fatigue. It was hard to rest. The world was full of wonders.

RASSUL RETURNED FROM his journey to Kashgar a changed man. He had seen the shifting sands of the Taklamakan Desert and fairy-tale castles made of stone. Back in Leh, the fine new clothes he had purchased in Kashgar marked him as a man who had seen the world. "With those clothes seemed myself as a big babu," he chuckled to himself as he looked back, "on whole body was like English." He bought exotic souvenirs—a samovar and "Russian clothes"—for his wife and mother and never missed an opportunity to tell the story of his latest adventure. Still, he had mixed emotions about his new attire: "Sometimes felt much ashamed with those clothes. Sometimes felt was enjoy." Leh had changed in his absence, too, at least in Rassul's eyes. After his experiences on the open road, in the mountain passes, and in Yarkand and Kashgar, his hometown felt both smaller and more precious.

Such symbols of the explorer's status—foreign clothes, exotic souvenirs—were as important to guides and porters like Rassul Galwan as they were to the nominal leaders of their expeditions. When Younghusband reached the oasis town of Ya-hu after nine weeks in the Gobi Desert on a previous expedition, he was surprised to find that Ma-te-la, the Mongolian camel driver he had hired in Kwei-hwa-cheng, had been collecting odds and ends "such as bits of paper, ends of string, a worn-out sock" he associated with the expedition. At first, Younghusband could not comprehend why anyone would save what to his eyes was merely trash—that is, until he learned that Ma-te-la had family in Ya-hu. He had saved these souvenirs to show to his family. In his eyes and theirs, it was evidence of another world—and evidence that he was a man who had seen it for himself. He was an explorer, and he had proof.

The relief of home never lasted long for Rassul Galwan. Within weeks of returning, the homesickness of the road had been replaced by restlessness. He returned from his fourth expedition—a hunting trip deep into the Pamir Mountains with two Englishmen—with a deep well of new stories and experiences. He had met the Shamal people and watched as their trained falcons streaked down out of the sky onto the back of an unsuspecting rabbit. He had witnessed a Chinese funeral and Chinese New Year celebrations, complete with a "lion dance," where an enormous paper dragon seemed to come to life. "At that time I had not seen the like before," he recorded. "It seemed me very wonderful." He made careful notes of a boat made of paper to impress his neighbors back in Leh. Even the hunt itself had brought new experiences. He remembered the "very beautiful" stag shot by one of the Englishmen. "Never had I see that kind of animal," he wrote in his memoirs. After months of travel, he was eager to return to Leh and share all that he had seen. Before he even reached his door, however, he was told that his wife had died while he was gone.

For several weeks, all his memories seemed tainted: the "hard wind" and stinging snow of the Mustagh Pass, the sprawling glacier that in the right light looked for all the world like a landscape dotted with shimmering Buddhist stupas, the pure relief of leaving the pass behind and descending into a green and forested valley that made it feel as though they had traveled from winter into summer in a single day, the cragged wreath of impossibly high peaks crested by a numinous "hat of cloud" ("I said to myself: 'Lucky man . . . to see that mountain'"), even drinking brandy to keep warm. While he had basked in these joys, his wife had sickened. He should have been by her side in Leh. The world had moved on without him.

He remarried quickly despite his sorrow; he needed a lodestone to guide him home. He gave a wedding feast for all his friends and replicated the paper boat he had seen at the Chinese New Year celebrations in Yarkand. He felt proud to bring a part of his travels, a part of the outside world, back home. He even promised his new wife that he would finally cease his endless wandering and put down roots in Leh. "My thought was that I would live a year with my good wife," he explained. "I wanted to travel a long way to look at other countries; but now I liked more to live in Leh, and was very happy."

But within days of his marriage and his promise, word arrived from Kashgar about a party of English travelers looking for guides to take them through the Himalayas to the mysterious Tibetan city of Lhasa. Though politically independent from Tibet, Ladakh was tied to the mountain kingdom by bonds of culture and religion. Most Ladakhis were Tibetan Buddhists, and it seemed every hill and cliff in the valley was topped by one of the splendid whitewashed Lamaist temples that appeared to cascade down to the valley floor. Indeed, though a Muslim himself, Rassul had grown up in the shadow of Leh's Buddhist temple and had long been fascinated by Buddhist art and rituals. When he heard that an expedition was preparing to travel to the very heart of Tibetan culture, Rassul could not resist. His mind once more filled with dreams of all that he might see: "many interesting countries," to be sure, but perhaps even a "railway and steamer." So he said farewell to his dejected wife and set out for Kashgar. As he gazed back at Leh for the last time from the top of the Kardong Pass, he "felt sorry and happy also."

Rassul's Tibet expedition of 1895 took him into uncharted territory. Lhasa, the Tibetan capital, was off-limits to Europeans. Even setting foot inside Tibet's closely guarded borders brought risk of death. In nearly four hundred years of Himalayan exploration, only a handful of Europeans had ever reached Lhasa, and none had seen the city with their own eyes for a generation. For explorers, the forbidden is often the most tantalizing. Rassul and his companions would not be diverted, even by the threat of death.

By 1895, Lhasa had become the aspiration of Asian exploration, the prize all ambitious explorers coveted above all else. St. George and Teresa Littledale, the leaders of the expedition, knew that previous attempts to sneak through Tibet to Lhasa had failed, turned back by suspicious Tibetans long before they reached the forbidden city. Some had even died trying. The Littledales hoped that the longer, more perilous route over the Tien Shan Mountains to Kashgar, then south across the desolate Chang Tang Plateau and into the Himalayas, would be overlooked. That path would also avoid the major caravan routes, so word of their party would not reach the ear of Lhasa. No one would suspect that anyone would risk entry from the north.

All went according to plan until they reached the Chang Tang. Raked by hail and thunderstorms in summer and arctic winds in winter, the high-altitude plateau seemed entirely devoid of life. It had few plants and little wildlife and was sparsely populated—only the nomadic Changpa called the region home. As the Littledales intended, they did not see a soul for months on end as they dragged themselves across the plain. At first they sang as they walked and spent the evenings keeping the growing feeling of isolation at bay with stories and songs of home. As they traveled farther into "this ocean of desert," the days, then weeks, blurred into an indistinct haze of dying donkeys and featureless plains. With the animals succumbing with alarming frequency—Rassul estimated that forty died in the crossing—they were forced to slow their progress to a few miles a day. This pace helped the animals but meant that their supplies were rapidly dwindling.

Many of Rassul's Ladakhi companions began to despair: they never should have joined this expedition. Rassul urged them to carry on. He was in charge of their supplies, and he was certain he had purchased enough to see them through. And besides, he told them, think of all the wonderful things they had seen, think of the stories they would tell their friends back home. "I hope we will find villages, and must come to Ladakh, by helping God, after some months. And will make many other journeys after this. Then will tell this story: 'When we was with Mr. Littledale, was that and this.'" He reminded them of the inquisitive antelope that had come so near because it had never seen people before and of the wild yaks, the first they'd ever seen; the Christmas feast given by George Macartney in Kashgar and the exotic dance they joined in Khotan. He for one would carry on. There was so much more to see.

As they crept closer to Lhasa, it became clear that their presence had been noticed. They were met by soldiers and officials from Lhasa who insisted they turn back. As they passed the holy lake of Tengri Nor and entered the Goring Valley a few days march from Lhasa, they were met by more senior officials bearing warnings from the capital. Then Mrs. Littledale fell ill. Mr. Littledale finally bowed to the ever-increasing threats from the Tibetans. They had come closer to Lhasa than any European had come in decades, only to stumble at the last hurdle.

They crossed back into Ladakh at Durga. Rassul was "pleased to arrived own country." That night, they were feted by their countrymen with music, dancing, and singing late into the night. The next day they would be home. When the new day dawned at last, they donned new attire purchased in Tibet for this very purpose. They wanted to make an entrance into Leh worthy of world travelers.

Their hearts sang as Leh came into view. Even twenty years later, Rassul found it hard to find the words to express his feelings: "At that time, how shall I write? Every one traveller know this happy; after long journey, reaching at home." When he at last arrived at his own door, he found his wife and his mother there to greet him. "When see me, laughed, and said: 'Welcome.' I said: 'By help of God, and with your right prayer, I came well.'" Friends and neighbors gathered to see the man who they had given up for dead. "Now that night was a very happy night," Rassul remembered, so full of happy tears and laughter. "Was so pleased I cannot tell all that happy." In his mind, however, he was already planning his next journey, a short expedition to Kashmir. He would leave the next day.

There would be more journeys in Rassul Galwan's future. He led another English hunting expedition into western China, guided the Harvard professor Roland Dixon and the Italian scientist Fillipo Fillipi across the mountains and onto the Asian steppe, and joined several expeditions with the American explorer Robert Barrett, who helped him put the story of his life into writing. As he labored over each page of his narrative, the memories of all he had seen came flooding back. He was now a man with a family and a stable position in Leh. He had much to keep him there and much to risk if he left again to wander. Even then, he could not help but dream of the wonderful new worlds that might yet swim into his ken.

AS THEY HACKED THEIR way through the dense forest of the Tumen River valley on the border between Korea and Manchuria in April 1912, the porters grumbled that they had not signed up for this. Indeed, most of the party had not signed up for anything at all. The young American naturalist who led the expedition had arrived at Ulsan, on the southern tip of Japanese-occupied Korea, to investigate the existence of a supposedly extinct species of whale. When the whaling season closed in March, Roy Chapman Andrews turned his gaze farther north to the largely unexplored region between the Tumen and Yalu Rivers, where his boyhood hero, Sir Francis Younghusband, had made his name as an explorer: an uncharted land of "treacherous swamps, forested plateaus, and gloomy cañons—a vast wilderness treasuring in its depths the ghostly peak of the Long White Mountain, wonderfully beautiful in its robes of glistening pumice." There a crater lake nestled like glistening jade in a forest of larch. Andrews was eager to make his own mark, and this was the perfect backdrop for his first foray into the romantic world of exploration.

In Seoul, Andrews recruited a Japanese interpreter fluent in Korean and a Korean cook named Kim. In Musan, in the north, he added a legendary tiger hunter named Paik to the crew and five horsemen, or *mafoos*, chosen by the commander of the Japanese garrison and ordered to join the expedition. The area around the Long White Mountain was believed by locals to be a haunted realm of bandits and demons. No one in Musan, apart from Paik, had volunteered to join Andrews's expedition.

The farther north they traveled, the worse the conditions became. The "forest became so thick we had to cut our way through the tangled branches," Andrews remembered. "All the party came under the influence of the gloom and silence, and it was difficult to make them proceed." Constant downpours soaked them to the bone and transformed the ground beneath their feet into a sucking, slipping quagmire. At times it became so impassable that they were forced to cut down trees to form makeshift bridges to help the horses across the muck. Without these bridges, the horses sank up to their stomachs. Day after day, they struggled beneath a canopy so dense that it clouded out the sun, leaving the weary party in a world of perpetual twilight, clinging damp, and unremitting cold. "The silence . . . of the forest began to work upon the Koreans," Andrews recorded, "and after we had been threading our way for five days through the mazes of an untouched wilderness the natives were discouraged and asked to return."

The mafoos had had enough. They discussed refusing to go one step further into this nightmarish forest. The building fatigue and resentment disappeared, however, when they caught their first glimpse of the sacred slopes of Paektu, the Long White Mountain, peeking through the screen of larch branches. The mountain played a starring role in their history and folklore. In their history, this mountain was the birthplace of Dangun, the legendary founder and god-king of Gojoseon, the first Korean kingdom. And now, here was the mythic mountain, rising stark and white out of an endless sea of trees. For weeks they had hardly been able to contain their frustration; now they could hardly contain their joy. "Banked to the top with snow, it looked like a great white cloud that had settled to earth for a moment's rest," Andrews wrote. "The open sky and the mountain acted like magic on my men. They began to talk and sing and call to each other in laughing voices."

For Andrews, the Long White Mountain meant adventure and accomplishment. For the Koreans, it meant something more profound. In the midst of Japanese occupation, this was the place that, more than any other, symbolized Korean identity and resistance. And though they had not sought it out, the mafoos had now seen this birthplace of the Korean people for themselves.

Unlike Rassul Galwan, the Korean mafoos did not leave an account of their travels in their own words. Like so many of the men and women who guided and carried the great expeditions of the nineteenth century, they have largely been erased from the historical record. Even their names have been forgotten. But this does not mean that their experiences have been lost entirely; something of their lives still survives in the accounts of men like Roy Chapman Andrews and Henry Morton Stanley. If we look closely at such texts, we can resurrect explorers like Chuma and Susi and the Korean mafoos and begin to understand their experiences, the suffering and the wonder, the toil and the curiosity.

CHAPTER 6

MIGRATION

———

BY THE EARLY years of the twentieth century, it seemed to many as if there were no more new worlds to discover. The poles had been conquered and every blank spot on the map in between filled in, bound by telegraph and telephone, steamship and railway. The age of exploration was closed. And yet, discovery is not limited to venturing into the physical unknown. Some of the greatest expeditions involve people discovering new lives for themselves, whether driven by dreams or need or want or war to find a new homeland. The steamship, the railroad, and communications by telegraph all helped to bring about an unprecedented increase in human migration, with millions moving across the globe, encountering new peoples and exploring new ways of life.

THE VOYAGE TO New England was an unmooring experience for thirteen-year-old Mary Antin. In the middle of the Atlantic, she was caught between two worlds. Behind her in the east was the old world of her childhood, the world of home and history, but also of religious tension and persecution, even mass murder in the brutal pogroms of the Russian Pale of Settlement. To the west, where the ship's prow pointed, was the New World, the world of hope and uncertainty, the world of the future.

The open ocean was an eerie place, at once terrifying and enchanting. The light, the air, the very ground beneath her feet, seemed changeable and contingent. The ship moved constantly, rocking and swaying in every direction all at once as if in a drunken stupor. At first, it was difficult to stand, let alone sleep as the ship pitched and rolled, pitched and rolled, with no prospect of relief. "I tried to fall asleep," another voyager remembered, "but the ship was rocking like a seesaw, and all the utensils kept banging against the wall in a musical rhythm that was simply deafening." It didn't help that the atmosphere below deck was stultifying, "dreadful, salty, suffocating," in the words of one traveler. Mary spent the first week at sea lying with seasickness, clutching at her bed in a desperate attempt to make the world stop spinning. She wondered if she would ever feel well again.

Eventually, Mary's body became attuned to the motion of the waves. Climbing out of the hold and onto the deck was like coming up for air: a burst of brilliant light, the bite of the wind, and the tang of salt on the breeze. But relief was mixed with the dislocating effect of the open ocean. The ship seemed tiny here, at the mercy of nature, exposed and utterly helpless, especially when the sea was rough. Mary's ship was fortunate to avoid the worst tempests of the North Atlantic, but even a small storm was terrifying. "The whole sea was an expanse of mountainous waves," a contemporary wrote, "the ship was battered about like a splinter, up one wave and down another." "It was frightening to see huge waves black as ink which appeared ready to swallow the entire ship," another voyager remembered of his first glimpse of an angry sea. "Everything on deck was covered with ice. . . . Everyone in our quarters was very frightened. . . . The women were crying. The men gathered together and were reciting psalms." Only God knew whether they would ever reach America.

When the sea was calm and fear subsided, the crossing could be wondrous. "In the evenings, when the sky was clear, we would gaze at the enchanting colors of sunset—gaze and give vent to our rapture," one voyager recalled. The setting sun seemed to guide them to the promise of the New World, leading them to a bright future. "Then, as the magical hues extinguished themselves one by one, our hearts would reach out with longing." At such times, there was laughter and dancing, songs of home and dreamy discussion of their new lives beyond the far horizon. It helped that Mary had her family with her.

The Antins were not the only ones heading for America. By the 1880s, hundreds of thousands of Jews from the Baltic to the Black Sea were fleeing destruction of their homes, lives, and businesses and making for the border to escape the pogroms. Like many of their neighbors, the Antins sought a place where they would be free to live without the fear of persecution. "The word 'America' was heard more than any other," another Jewish migrant of the era wrote. It "had for them a special kind of magnetism, a kind of magical meaning. It stood for an ideal of which many, many had long dreamed . . . a kind of heaven, a sort of Paradise." "America was in everybody's mouth," Mary remembered. "Business men talked of it over their accounts; the market women made up their quarrels that they might discuss it from stall to stall; people who had relatives in the famous land went around reading their letters for the enlightenment of less fortunate folks . . . children played at emigrating; old folks shook their sage heads over the evening fire, and prophesied no good for those who braved the terrors of the sea and the foreign goal beyond it." By 1891, Mary's father had left for this new world.

Mary and the rest of the family followed in the spring of 1894. From their home in Polotsk, in what is now Belarus, they traveled through Lithuania and crossed into Germany at Eydtkunen (modern Chernyshevskoye). There was no room to move in the crowded train that barreled along to Berlin. For days, Mary, her mother, and her three sisters sat perched atop their luggage without sleep. After a lifetime in the small village of Polotsk, the vertiginous swirl of Berlin was exhilarating for Mary. She had always dreamed of Paris or Vienna or Berlin, and now, here she was. The "splendid houses, stone and brick, and showy shops," the electric trolley and the crowds, everything about the world beyond Belarus was fascinating to Mary. After Berlin, the Antin women continued to Hamburg, where they crowded into a lodging house and waited for two agonizing weeks before they at last found a place on a ship heading for America. In April 1894, they boarded the *Polynesia* and began their fateful crossing.

They had been at sea for seventeen days when the New World appeared. It was May, and the weather was full of gentle promise. Everyone on board the *Polynesia* was pressed expectantly against the ship's rail, hoping to catch a first glimpse of New England. "Oh Joyful sight!" Mary recorded. "We saw the tops of two trees!" Everyone was shouting with unconstrained excitement. As the shore drew near, a verdant land materialized. For Mary, it was everything she imagined the new Canaan to be. "Oh what a beautiful scene!" she wrote. "No corner of the earth is half so fair as the lovely picture before us. It came to view suddenly—a green field, a real field with grass on it, and large houses, and the dearest hens and little chickens in all the world, and trees, and birds, and people at work."

"Oh. It's our turn at last!" Mary Antin wrote of her landing in Boston Harbor and her reunion with her father. "A rush over the planks . . . over the ground . . . six wild beings cling to each other, bound by a common bond of tender joy, and the long parting is at an END." Now the Antins faced the strange rituals of American immigration—the snaking lines, the endless waiting, the intrusive questions and invasive medical examinations, and the constant, countless misunderstandings. "Why so many ceremonies at

The immigrants who passed through Castle Garden immigration station in Battery Park, New York (the precursor to Ellis Island) were among the millions of immigrant explorers whose journeys reshaped the globe in the nineteenth and twentieth centuries. (National Gallery of Art, Corcoran Collection; Museum Purchase, Gallery Fund)

the landing?" a weary Mary wondered. It was the first of many odd things Mary and her fellow immigrant explorers would encounter in this new land.

IMMIGRANTS LIKE MARY ANTIN are rarely thought of as explorers. But their own accounts of their journeys prove that their experiences and those more usually recognized as "exploration" need to be considered together. By the early twentieth century, more and more migrants were recording their experiences, and in their narratives we can hear the language of discovery. Their motivations for leaving home were often brutal and coerced—and so, too, were the beginnings of many of the stories we have already heard. As they wrote, they did not downplay the horrors they had left or the bigotry they encountered in their new homes. But they also explicitly and deliberately imagined themselves as discovering the world. Acknowledging this is not about romanticizing migration: it is, instead, allowing immigrants to speak for themselves, to take their experiences seriously.

IN THE TWENTIETH CENTURY, even as the world was racked by two global wars and the borders of nations hardened, migration became easier and cheaper for the millions who set out in search of opportunity. Theirs were journeys of discovery too.

At twenty years of age, Allyson Williams was settling into a comfortable life in Port of Spain, the capital of Trinidad and Tobago. Her childhood had been a happy one, full of laughter and music and family. She had done well at school and had already been promoted twice at her job at the Ministry of Education. It was a lifetime position. She was the envy of her classmates. Her future was secure. And yet, one year later, at twenty-one, Allyson would trade her stable life in Trinidad for an uncertain future a world away.

As a schoolgirl, Allyson had daydreamed of becoming an interpreter at the United Nations headquarters in New York, and she knew friends and neighbors whose ancestors had come to the Caribbean from every corner of the globe—Africa, India, Syria, China. Her father even worked at the nearby American naval base. She knew much about the world beyond Trinidad. And yet, in 1967, she assumed that the outside world would remain a distant dream. It thus came as a surprise to everyone, Allyson included, when word of a nursing shortage in Britain captured her imagination and changed the course of her life.

Britain had emerged from World War II a shell of its former self. Its economy was in tatters. Labor was in short supply. Immigrants were desperately needed to fill the labor void and help rebuild the country. The first of these immigrants to arrive in Britain in 1948 were recruited from across the Caribbean—Jamaica, Barbados, Grenada, St. Lucia—and transported across the Atlantic aboard the HMS *Empire Windrush*. Over the next three decades, thousands more would follow from the West Indies, Africa, and other areas of the British Commonwealth, drawn to the possibility of a better life in Britain. Collectively, they came to be known as the Windrush generation.

Trinidad had more than its share of members of the Windrush generation, so when Allyson learned of an opportunity to join them, she was determined to follow their path to Britain. Her mother was a nurse and midwife, so Allyson could at least draw on her professional expertise as she prepared to make her journey. And she knew plenty about Britain, too. Britain was far from an unknown quantity for people throughout the Commonwealth. "England was foremost in our minds and in our heads and in our hearts," Allyson remembered. "Everything we did . . . everything we learned about, all the kings and queens . . . English literature, everything. Everything was about the mother country. . . . So it was all there in our heads all the time. My thoughts were that I would go and explore and see what it was all about, and then come straight back home. . . . I thought I would be a pioneer and go to England."

As Allyson Williams quickly learned, however, the migrant experience was not all wide-eyed wonder and dreams fulfilled. Like other explorers, migrants assessed their surroundings with a critical eye, weighing and measuring the reality of their new environments with the stories of foreign lands that had inspired their choice of destination. What they found could be jarring, not just because it was different from home—that was to be expected—but because their new homes often failed to live up to the image they had in mind. When she arrived in London to take her place as a trainee nurse at Whittington Hospital in 1968, Allyson was overcome with disappointment. "I was shocked when I came to London," she later admitted. "It was so dull and so dark. I didn't know at the time that that was how British cities were built, with all these houses joined on to each other. It was just quite depressing . . . and difficult to conceptualize." Many new arrivals, on seeing the cramped row houses black with soot, chimneys belching dark clouds of pungent coal smoke, assumed that they were factories. How could this be where the British, the wealthiest of peoples, really lived? She had expected the glamor of Buckingham Palace, not grim and gritty postwar London. She "cried for about three months solidly because it was so dark and grey" and began to think, "this is not the mother country—what happened to this place?"

She made an expensive overseas call to her mother in tears and told her she wanted to come home to Trinidad. Her mother reminded her that she had not gone to England "to like the place" but to improve her life. She should stick it out until her training was complete. Over time, Allyson's perspective began to change. She still found England "dark," "depressing," and "dismal," but as she learned more about the country, she began to understand it, to realize "why it looks like it does." And as her outlook changed, she began to make friends with other immigrants, and together they explored their new surroundings. "We would go and explore the Underground," Allyson recalled. "We didn't know how to read the signs or anything, so we would just jump on a train . . . and that's how we started." They explored Kensington, Harrods department store, and Madame Tussauds wax museum. Before long, Allyson herself felt like she had "become the icon in London" for people arriving from the West Indies, the guide and point of reference for each new wave of immigrants from home.

The same was true of the thousands of Chinese explorers who ventured to California, Australia, and South Africa and of immigrants of all stripes throughout the ages. Those who blazed the trail from Russia to New York or from Trinidad to London were pioneers and explorers just as much as those who braved the mountains of California or the Australian outback. Indeed, recent studies have shown that immigrants often possess traits usually reserved for explorers and pioneers: they tend to be more autonomous, more independent minded, more goal oriented, and more restless than those who stay. Anne Sofie Beck Knudsen's work on Scandinavian immigrants found that those who immigrated to America in the nineteenth century were more likely to share various markers of individualism. Many of them might have seen something of themselves in the accounts of explorers.

IN HIS OLD AGE, Ezekiel Perez recalled the stories of the first people from his pueblo to make the journey north. Three men, their names still remembered more than half a century later, had set out on foot from Las Barrancas in 1914, heading for the gold mines near Sacramento, California. The impression they made on their return ensured that generations of young people would associate el Norte with wealth and opportunity. According to Perez, Santiago Gonzales came back to the pueblo "all dressed up, wearing a suit of pure cashmere," spending extravagantly on mariachis and tequila for his godchildren's wedding. Every town and village in northern Mexico had their own Santiago Gonzales, a traveler who set out for the North and came back rich, and over the decades that followed, millions would follow in their footsteps and heed the call of el Norte. Folk ballads (corridos) celebrating these explorers became a staple throughout the country, sung on street corners and played over the radio, ensuring that generations of Mexicans heard stories of the North.

In 1986, four men would stand on a hill above Tijuana, inheritors of this tradition, drawn to el Norte like so many of their forebearers. They had been raised on stories of streets paved with gold, of fortunes made and lives forever changed. In his late twenties, Leonardo came to Tijuana to seek work across the border in California, where the pay was better. Forty-five-year-old Enrique came because in the town where he lived, he could never quite support his family, no matter how hard he worked. But like so many Mexicans before them, the draw of el Norte was not only about money. Roberto, at twenty the youngest of the four, hoped to find work in el Norte, but in his heart dreamed of something more, something ineffable yet deeply human. He wanted to break free from the familiar and journey into the unknown. "Yes, of course I want to work and make some money," he readily admitted to a reporter, "but the real reason is to know more about the world. For many years now I have studied about the United States, and now I want to have the adventure and see for myself." For many, the voyage has become a rite of passage and the experience of the world beyond as important as the money to be made. José Vasquez Ordaz went north because his father had done so "and I too wanted to have the adventure." Like his father, Ordaz came back with life-changing money and a wealth of stories that he would tell and retell for the rest of his days. "It was," he said after his return to Mexico from California, "a grand adventure that year."

WE CAN'T DOWNPLAY THE awful forces that drive migration—poverty, corruption, violence, environmental crisis. But in focusing solely on the physical and material, we sometimes miss the role imagination and adventure play in deciding who will head out for parts unknown. Every year across the world, millions of people migrate, not all of them in terror or desperate need. Many do so because they have no other option. But to pursue safety or a better life requires the ability to imagine that such a life exists, somewhere beyond the horizon.

CONNECTION

———

"I THINK I'M THE first man to sit on top of the world," Matthew Henson bellowed to Commodore Robert Peary as he tromped back into camp with Ootah and Ooqueah. For years, the North Pole had been the ultimate prize in exploration, one of the last places on earth that humankind had yet to reach. Dozens of expeditions had joined the race. Hundreds had died in the attempt. And now, on April 7, 1909, three men became the first humans to plant their feet on the roof of the world: two Inughuit Inuit and an African American sharecropper's son from Maryland.

There is nothing unusual about such diversity in the annals of exploration. When Lewis and Clark first reached the Pacific, an enslaved African man named York and a Shoshone woman named Sacagawea were at their sides. When Austen Henry Layard uncovered cuneiform tablets containing the *Epic of Gilgamesh* at Nineveh in the 1850s, he was aided by an Assyrian archaeologist named Hormuzd Rassam. When Robert Burke and William Wills made the first cross-continental journey through the parched Australian outback in 1860–61, they were led by a pair of Muslim camel

drivers from Afghanistan and Pakistan and two Indian camel driv-
ers, one Hindu, one Parsi. Their expedition would have surely per-
ished without Dost Mahomet, Esau Khan, Samla, and Belooch
Khan. The source of the Nile was discovered by Richard Francis
Burton, John Hanning Speke, *and* Mubarak Bombay and Mabruki.
The last two were at Henry Morton Stanley's side when he greeted
Dr. Livingstone in 1871. Hiram Bingham III discovered Machu
Picchu in 1911 after being led to the site by a local guide named
Melchor Arteaga. When Sir Edmund Hillary climbed atop Mt.
Everest in May of 1959, he shared the triumph with a Nepalese
Sherpa named Tenzing Norgay. Exploration has always been a mat-
ter of human connection. Matthew Henson, Ootah, and Ooqueah
were in good company.

Henson's journey to the Arctic Circle began in 1867 at the age
of one, when his parents were forced to flee their farm in Charles
County, Maryland, by white vigilantes in the days after the American Civil War. In Georgetown, where the family settled, Henson
had access to a wider range of role models and was inspired by a
speech by Frederick Douglass to go out into the world and uplift his
race. At twelve, Henson could sit still no longer and made for the
busy port of Baltimore, where he signed on as a cabin boy on ships
sailing to Africa, China, and Japan.

He had already seen more of the world than most Americans
when a naval officer strode into the B. H. Stinemetz & Son clothing store in Georgetown in 1887 and changed his life. Robert Peary
was a man of bottomless ambition and sensed a connection with the
young Black salesclerk who had already traveled to the far side of the
world by the age of twenty-one. Peary was outfitting a naval expedition to scout potential paths for a transcontinental canal through

Nicaragua and offered Henson a place at his side before he even left the store. Henson leapt at the chance to see a new corner of the globe.

Deep in the jungles of Nicaragua, Peary confided to Henson his dream of making his name as a polar explorer, the heroes of the day. Henson made the dream his own.

Their first expedition to Greenland in 1891–92 taught the pair how much they did not know about the brutal conditions at the poles. But unlike most explorers of their time, they were willing to listen to the people who knew how to travel and survive in the icy North. In the Middle Ages, the Inuits' ancestors, the Thule, had made the journey from coastal Alaska across the top of Canada to Greenland, where they ran headlong into the Dorset people and Viking explorers from Scandinavia. By the nineteenth century, the Inuit had a millennium of experience with Arctic voyaging. Henson and Peary traded their European wools for fur clothing and hired Inuit guides and hunters. They learned the language and studied Inuit techniques for building igloos and traveling by dogsled. Without the need for heavy tents and sleeping bags, they could travel lighter, faster, and farther than most of their Western rivals. After two further expeditions to the Arctic, they were ready to make their dash for the North Pole.

They left New York in the hazy heat of July 1908 and steamed north aboard the *Roosevelt* to Cape York, Greenland, where they recruited twenty-two Inuit men and seventeen women as hunters, dogsled handlers, and clothing makers before continuing north. The open sea was a new experience for the Inuit. They were expert ocean travelers, but knew that in the unpredictable Arctic, it was best to keep close to shore. The absence of land was unsettling.

By April 1, 1909, only six men remained out on the ever-shifting
sea ice north of Ellesmere Island. Some members of the expedition
had remained behind on the *Roosevelt* to await their return. Others
had carried supplies to the camp just 132 miles south of the pole
before turning back. All that was left now was for Henson, Peary,
Egingwah, Seeglo, Ootah, and Ooqueah to make the final push
for glory.

Henson had handpicked the crucial party. Seeglo and the brothers Ootah and Egingwah were old hands at exploration, and Henson trusted their expertise and unflappable sangfroid. Ooqueah, the
youngest, was on his first Peary expedition, but like the others, he was
a skilled dog handler, "the best in the tribe" in Henson's estimation.
And Henson was an excellent judge. He spoke the Inuit language,
had been given an affectionate Inuit name—Mahri-Pahluk—and
had a son with an Inuit woman named Akatingwah. He even made
the sleds himself to an Inuit design.

The six men struck out for the pole on April 1—"It was All
Fools Day," Henson reflected, "but the coincidence did not worry
us." For days they picked their way north across the ice, clamber-
ing over or hacking through the jagged tumble of pressure ridges
formed where two sheets of ice collided. They navigated breaks in
the ice by converting icebergs into makeshift "ferryboats," pad-
dling across sea channels with their snowshoes. The ice was no
smooth sheet, but it was lifeless and monotonous. The sun never
left the sky, but its constant presence was not a comfort. There
was "no warmth in its rays," Henson remembered. Night and day
were merely divisions of time marked by a watch, rather than a
discernable reality. There was rest, but no relief from the blinding
white, no sitting around the campfire, no campfire at all. It was

maddening. The wind was somehow worse. It, too, was ever-present, ever-pummeling, the only thing that seemed alive. It drove granulated snow into their faces at temperatures of –15 to –59 Fahrenheit, freezing and scouring their skin until it peeled off "like raw beef." At "night" they constructed igloos, ate tea and biscuits and pemmican, and went right to sleep, waking up frozen stiff every few hours as a light snow rained down on them, their frozen breath falling back to earth.

April 7 dawned clear and cold at –33. They thought they were

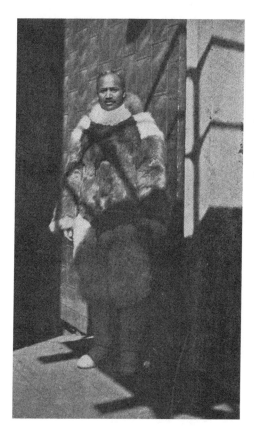

In 1909, Matthew Henson, the son of sharecroppers from Maryland, was the first person to reach the North Pole alongside the Inuit explorers Seeglo, Ootah, Egingwah, and Ooqueah. (National Portrait Gallery, Smithsonian Institution)

close to the pole and "expectation was written on every face" in anticipation of Peary's measurements at noon. They would know "at last whether we had reached our goal." While Peary worked out their position, Henson, Ootah, and Ooqueah reconnoitered. Peary's calculations were inconsistent and suggested that they were either very near the pole or had crossed it earlier in their journey. Henson, Ootah, and Ooqueah doubled back to the likely spot. When they arrived, Henson "could see that my footprints were the first" to reach it. They hurried back to camp to tell Peary they had done it. Henson, Ootah, and Ooqueah had reached the pole.

There was "no riotous outburst of feeling," Henson reported, "a temperature of 50 degrees below zero is pretty close to the freezing point of sentiment." They planted an American flag, and Henson and the four Inuit posed for a picture. Henson then called for three cheers in Inuit. The Inuit were "jumping around and exclaiming: 'Ting neigh tima ketisher!' which means, 'We have reached here at last!'" Though they would appear in few of the accounts of the Peary expedition's triumph, the wonder of their accomplishment was not lost on the Inuit explorers. Nor was it lost on Henson. "As I stood there at the top of the world and thought of the hundreds of men who had lost their lives in the effort to reach it, I felt profoundly grateful that I . . . had the honor of representing my race in the historic achievement." Africa, Europe, and Indigenous America had united on the roof of the world.

IN 1987, AN INUIT MAN stood side by side with an African American actress in Woodlawn Cemetery in the Bronx to pay their respects to an explorer. Anaukaq had traveled all the way from Greenland to lay a wreath on the grave of a man he never knew, his father, Matthew Henson, the first man to reach the North Pole. Taraji P. Henson was his distant relation. Two branches of an African, American, Inuit family—two branches of the human family—reunited through exploration.

It might seem as though the age of exploration had closed by the time Anaukaq reached his father's grave, that his solemn vigil marked the passing of a man and the passing of an era. By 1987, the South Pole had been conquered, Everest had been summited not just once but thousands of times, and even the moon bore the mark of several sets of human footprints. In a time when the entire world seems to be at one's fingertips, when anyone can call up anything with the press of a button, when the earth is wrapped in waves and wires and mapped to the inch by GPS, it might seem as though there is nothing left to discover. But exploration is a timeless, universal impulse. Discovery is infinite. It is, and always has been, a question of perspective.

Anaukaq was following in his father's footsteps when he traveled to New York in 1987 to investigate a world and a family he knew only from pictures. His son Vittus and his grandchildren Aviaq and Allen Anaukaq Matthew Henson continued the family tradition of exploration when they made the journey north from Nuuk to the edge of the Arctic Circle in 2009 to commemorate the centenary of Matthew Henson's celebrated expedition. None of Henson's descendants were the first to blaze the trail they followed; all sought to better understand the farthest reaches of their world, to expand their horizons and fill in the blank spaces on their maps, to explore. They, and thousands of other everyday explorers like them, demonstrate that exploration is still possible. It is not relegated to a previous age, nor is it the preserve of a privileged few who buy their way to the bottom of the ocean or the top of Everest or even into space. Exploration is for everyone who reaches beyond themselves with curiosity and imagination, who sets off into the unknown with a sense of wonder and a spirit of adventure. It is the inheritance of us all.

ACKNOWLEDGMENTS

Writing this book has been a journey of its own, with many people to thank.

The team at W. W. Norton has been extraordinary. My thanks to Alane Mason, Justin Cahill, and Caroline Adams for their exceptional vision, perceptive edits, and unflagging commitment to the project. I would also like to express my sincere gratitude to everyone at Norton who worked on the book, from the design team that produced a more beautiful book than I ever could have imagined to the production team that copyedited and proofread the book with such careful attention to detail. Thank you all.

At A.M. Heath, Bill Hamilton and the entire staff have been tireless in their support of my work, and I cannot thank them enough.

The University of Alabama has been a warm and generative home these past six years, and the Department of History full of kind, thoughtful, and intellectually stimulating colleagues and students: thank you to all.

As always, my thanks go to my family: Jack, Nancy, Jackson, Kaleb, John, Candice, Joey, and Josh Lockwood; Donald Kaufman and Wendy Moffat; Emma and Nina Kaufman and Eric and Henry Gardiner; Nell and Tess, who explored the world with me; and Lucy, who is typing these acknowledgments as we set off on another adventure.

NOTES ON SOURCES AND QUOTATIONS

CHAPTER 1: IMAGINING

For the history of early human diffusion, see Felipe Fernández-Armesto, *Pathfinders: A Global History* (New York: W. W. Norton, 2006), 1–14.

For the *Epic of Gilgamesh*, see Sophus Helle, *Gilgamesh: A New Translation of the Ancient Epic* (New Haven: Yale University Press, 2021).

For *The Odyssey*, see Homer, *The Odyssey*, trans. Robert Fagles (New York: Penguin, 1999).

For information on Himilco and Hanno, see Barry Cunliffe, *Europe between the Oceans: Themes and Variations, 9000 BC–AD 1000* (New Haven: Yale University Press, 2008). For Phytheas, see Barry Cunliffe, *The Extraordinary Voyage of Phytheas the Greek* (New York: Penguin, 2003).

The quote from Mansa Musa comes from Nehemia Levtzion and J. F. P. Hopkins, eds., *Corpus of Early Arabic Sources for West African History* (Princeton, NJ: Markus Wiener Publishers, 2000), 268–69.

The information and quotes relating to Faxian come from Faxian, *A Record of Buddhistic Kingdoms*, trans. James Legge (Oxford: Clarendon Press, 1886).

For Xuanzang, see Joanna Waley-Cohen, *The Sextants of Beijing: Global Currents in Chinese History* (New York: W. W. Norton, 2000).

For more on travel and exploration in ancient and early medieval Eurasia, see Peter Frankopan, *Silk Roads: A New History of the World* (London: Bloomsbury, 2015), 1–62; Valerie Hansen, *The Silk Road: A New History* (Oxford: Oxford University Press, 2012); Valerie Hansen, *The Year 1000: When Explorers Connected the World and Globalization Began* (New York: Scribner, 2020).

The story of Gudrid Far-Traveler and Freydís Eiríksdóttir is drawn from Keneva Kunz, trans., *The Vinland Sagas* (New York: Penguin Books, 2008). For the quote on the motivations of Scandinavian explorers, see Fernández-Armesto, *Pathfinders*, 54. For more on women and Scandinavian explorations, see Nancy Marie Brown, *The Far Traveler: Voyages of a Viking Woman* (Boston: Houghton Mifflin Harcourt, 2007).

Information and quotes relating to Marco Polo are drawn from Manuel Komroff, ed., *The Travels of Marco Polo* (New York: Random House, 2001).

For information and quotes on Rabban Bar Sauma, see E. A. Wallis Budge, trans., *The History of the Life and Travels of Rabban Sawma* (London: Harrison & Sons, 1928).

For more on pilgrims and travelers in medieval Eurasia, see Peter Frankopan, *Silk Roads*, 132–311.

For more on China and the world in the Middle Ages, see Waley-Cohen, *The Sextants of Beijing*.

CHAPTER 2: NEW WORLDS

For information on Zheng He and the Ming treasure fleets, I consulted Louise Levathes, *When China Ruled the Seas: The Treasure Fleet of the Dragon Throne, 1405–1433* (Oxford: Oxford Unversity Press, 1997); Edward Dreyer, *Zheng He: China and the Oceans in the Early Ming Dynasty, 1405–1433* (London: Pearson Longman, 2006). For Ma Huan's narrative, see Peter Mancall, ed., *Travel Narratives from the Age of Discovery: An Anthology* (Oxford: Oxford University Press, 2006).

For the Taíno voyage to Spain and quotes on the Atlantic crossing, see the letter from Eugenio de Salazaar, in John Parry and Robert Keith, eds., *New Iberian World: A Documentary History of the Discovery and Settlement of Latin America to the Early 17th Century* (New York: Times Books, 1984), 431–40; Caroline Dodds Pennock, *On Savage Shores: How Indigenous Americans Discovered Europe* (New York: Knopf, 2023), 28, 38, 58–59; Stephen Greenblatt, *Marvelous Possessions: The Wonder of the New World* (Chicago: University of Chicago Press, 2017).

For information and quotes from Ota Gyuichi, *Shichō Koki*, and Yasuke, see J. S. A Elisonas and J. P. Lamers, trans., *The Chronicle of Lord Nobunaga* (Leiden, Netherlands: Brill Academic, 2011). For more information about Yasuke, see Thomas Lockley and Geoffrey Girard, *African Samurai: The True Story of Yasuke, a Legendary Black Warrior in Feudal Japan* (New York: Harlequin Books, 2019).

For Jesuit quotes on sixteenth-century Japan, see Michael Cooper, ed., *They Came to Japan: An Anthology of European Reports on Japan, 1543–1640* (Ann Arbor: University of Michigan Center for Japanese Studies, 1995), 66.

For the Tenshō embassy, see Duarte de Sande, *De Missione Legatorum Iaponensium ad Romanam Curiam Rebusque in Europa* (Macau, 1590); Derek Massarella, ed., and J. F. Moran, trans., *Japanese Travellers in Sixteenth Century Europe: A Dialogue Concerning the Mission of the Japanese Ambassadors to the Roman Curia (1590)* (London: Routledge, 2012).

For the story of Pocahontas, I consulted Paula Gunn Allen, *Pocahontas: Medicine Woman, Spy, Entrepreneur, Diplomat* (New York: HarperCollins, 2004); Camilla Townsend, *Pocahontas and the Powhatan Dilemma* (New York: Hill and Wang, 2005); Pennock, *On Savage Shores.*

On Yemmerrawanne and Bennelong, see Matthew Lockwood, *To Begin the World Over Again: How the American Revolution Devastated the Globe* (New Haven: Yale University Press, 2019); Jack Brook, "The Forlorn Hope: Bennelong and Yammerrawannie Go to England," *Australian Aboriginal Studies*, no. 1 (2001): 36–47.

For more on the First Fleet and firsthand accounts of early British colonialism in Australia, see Tom Keneally, *The Commonwealth of Thieves: The Story of the Founding of Australia* (New York: Random House, 2006); John Dann, ed., *The Nagle Journal: A Diary of the Life of Jacob Nagle, Sailor, from the Year 1775 to 1841* (London: Weidenfeld and Nicolson, 1988); Paul Fidlon and R. J. Ryan, eds., *The Journal of Arthur Bowes-Smyth: Surgeon, Lady Penrhyn 1787–1789* (Sydney: Australian Documents Library, 1979); George Worgan, *Journal of a First Fleet Surgeon* (Sydney: Library Council of New South Wales, 1978); Watkin Tench, *A Complete Account of the Settlement at Port Jackson* (London: G. Nico and J. Sewell, 1793).

CHAPTER 3: EXCHANGE

For Mary Wortley Montagu's narrative and quotes, see Elizabeth Bohls and Ian Duncan, eds., *Travel Writing, 1700–1830: An Anthology* (Oxford: Oxford University Press, 2009), 71, 73, 76, 77; Lady Mary Wortley Montagu, *Turkish Embassy Letters*, ed. Malcolm Jack (London: Virago Press, 1994); Mary Wortley Montagu, *Letters of the Right Honourable Mary Wortley Montagu, Written during Her Travels in Europe, Asia and Africa* (London: T. Becket and P. A. de Hondt, 1790).

For more on Orientalism and European views of the Middle East, see Edward Said, *Orientalism* (New York: Vintage Books, 1979); Jürgen Osterhammel, *Unfabling the East: The Enlightenment's Encounter with Asia* (Princeton: Princeton University Press, 2018). For a discussion of how women explorers used their experiences of India and the Muslim world to bolster campaigns for women's rights, see Rafia Zakaria, *Against White Feminism: Notes on Disruption* (New York: W. W. Norton, 2021).

For the story of and quotations about Joseph Banks and Tupaia, see Joseph Banks, *Journal of the Right Hon. Sir Joseph Banks*, ed. Joseph Hooker (London: Macmillan & Co., 1896), 108, 109, 110, 116, 124. For more on Banks, see Jordan Goodman, *Planting the World: Joseph Banks and His Collectors* (London: William Collins, 2021); Toby Musgrave, *The Multifarious Mr. Banks: From Botany Bay to Kew, the Natural Historian Who Shaped the World* (New Haven: Yale University Press, 2020). For information about Captain Cook's expedition, see James Cook, *The Journals of Captain Cook* (New York: Penguin Classics, 2000).

For more on Polynesian navigation and exploration, see Nicholas Thomas, *Islanders: The Pacific in the Age of Empire* (New Haven: Yale University Press, 2011); Nicholas Thomas, *Voyagers: The Settlement of the Pacific* (New York: Basic Books, 2021); Christina Thompson, *Sea People: The Puzzle of Polynesia* (New York: Harper, 2019).

For Ahutoru and his travels in France, see Louis-Antoine de Bougainville, *The Pacific Journal of Louis-Antoine de Bougainville 1767–1768*, trans. John Dunmore (London: Hakluyt Society, 2002).

For Cook's quote on the consequences of exploration, see J. C. Beaglehole, ed., *The Journals of Captain James Cook on his Voyages of Discovery*, vol. 2: *The Voyage of the Resolution and Adventure, 1772–1773* (Cambridge: Hakluyt Society, 1969), 174–75.

For Diderot's quote on Tahiti, see Denis Diderot, "Le supplément au voyage de Bougainville," *Œuvres*, ed. Jacques-André Naigeon (Paris: Desay et Déterville, 1798), vol. III, 382–84.

For Carlos Del Pino and the Humboldt expedition, see Alexander von Humboldt and Aimé Bonpland, *Personal Narrative of Travels to the Equinoctial Regions of the New Continent, during the Years 1799–1804*, trans. Helen Maria Williams (London: Longman, Hurst, Rees, Orme, and Brown, 1814), vol. II, 258, 355, 365, 375–78, 393, 398–99, vol. III, 4, 109, 110; Andrea Wulf, *The Invention of Nature: Alexander von Humboldt's New World* (New York: Knopf, 2015).

For the Aimé Bonpland quote, see Wulf, *The Invention of Nature*, 51.

For the narrative and quotes relating to Columbus's fourth voyage, see Paul Leicester Ford, ed., *Writings of Christopher Columbus* (New York: Charles L. Webster, 1892), 122–23, 125.

On Sacagawea and the Corps of Discovery, see James Ronda, *Lewis and Clark among the Indians* (Lincoln: University of Nebraska Press, 1984); David Lavender, *The Way to the Western Sea: Lewis and Clark across the Continent* (Lincoln: University of Nebraska Press, 1998); Robert McCracken Peck, " 'To Acquire

What Knowledge You Can': The Scientific Contributions of Lewis and Clark," *South Dakota History* 34, no. 1 (2004): 5–27; Alvin Josephy Jr., ed., *Lewis and Clark through Indian Eyes: Nine Indian Writers on the Legacy of the Expedition* (New York: Vintage, 2007); Sacagawea Project Board of the Mandan, Hidatsa, and Arikara Nation, *Our Story of Eagle Woman Sacagawea: They Got It Wrong* (Orange, CA: Paragon Agency, 2021).

For Quotes from William Clark, see Gary Moulton, ed., *The Definitive Journals of Lewis and Clark* (Lincoln: University of Nebraska Press, 2002): vol. 4, August 17, 1805; vol. 6, January 7, 1806.

For the story of John Edmonstone and Charles Darwin, see Charles Waterton, *Wanderings in South America* (London: Mawman, 1825); Charles Darwin, *The Autobiography of Charles Darwin 1809–1882* (London: John Murray, 1892; Darwin Correspondence Project, "Letter no. 22," accessed September 12, 2023, https://www.darwinproject.ac.uk/letter/DCP-LETT-22.xml; R. B. Freeman, "Darwin's Negro Bird-Stuffer," *Notes and Records of the Royal Society of London* 33, no.1 (August 1978).

CHAPTER 4: INTERPRETING

For the story of Dean Mahomet, see Dean Mahomet, *The Travels of Dean Mahomet: An Eighteenth-Century Journey through India*, ed. Michael Fisher (Berkeley: University of California Press, 1997), 34, 36–38, 60–62, 68–69, 72, 83–84, 124, 128–29, 130, 133; Lockwood, *To Begin the World Over Again*.

For Voltaire's quote on his play *Mahomet*, see Madeleine Kasten, "Staging the Barbarian: The Case of Voltaire's *Le Fanatisme, ou Mahomet le prohète*," *Thamyris/Intersecting*, no 29 (2015): 155.

For Henrietta Clive's quotes on India, see Henrietta Clive, *Birds of Passage: Henrietta Clive's Travels in South India, 1798–1801*, ed. Nancy Shields (London: Eland, 2016), 66–67, 90, 110.

For Eliza Fay's letters from India, see Eliza Fay, *Original Letters from India*, ed. E. M. Forster (New York: NYRB Classics, 2010), 202–3.

On **Mungo Park and the exploration of Africa,** see Mungo Park, *Travels in the Interior of Africa* (London: W. Bulmer and Co., 1799), 68–71, 82, 319.

For the travels of David Dorr, see David Dorr, *A Colored Man Round the World* (Cleveland, 1858). For more on African American travel in the antebellum period, see Elizabeth Stordeur Pryor, *Colored Travelers: Mobility and the Fight for Citizenship before the Civil War* (Chapel Hill: University of North Carolina Press, 2016).

For the quote from William Wells Brown on London, see William Wells Brown, *The American Fugitive in Europe: Sketches of Places and People Abroad* (Boston: John P. Jewett, 1855), 40–41. For more on fugitive slaves in Britain, see Matthew Lockwood, *Island Refuge: A History of Refugees in Britain* (London: HarperCollins, 2024).

CHAPTER 5: GUIDING

On **African exploration in the nineteenth century,** see Dane Kennedy, *The Last Blank Spaces: Exploring Africa and Australia* (Cambridge, MA: Harvard University Press, 2013); Robert Harms, *Land of Tears: The Exploration and Exploitation of Equatorial Africa* (New York: Basic Books, 2019); Tim Jeal, *Explorers of the Nile: The Triumph and Tragedy of a Great Victorian Adventure* (New Haven: Yale University Press, 2011); Candice Millard, *River of the Gods: Genius, Courage, Betrayal in the Search for the Source of the Nile* (New York: Doubleday, 2022).

For Henry Stanley's expedition, the "Faithfuls," and David Livingstone, see Henry Morton Stanley, *How I found Livingstone* (London: Scribner, Armstrong & Co., 1871); Tim Jeal, *Stanley: The Impossible Life of Africa's Greatest Explorer* (New Haven: Yale University Press, 2008); Martin Dugard, *Into Africa: The Epic Adventures of Stanley and Livingstone* (New York: Crown, 2004); Candice Millard, *River of the Gods.*

On **Chuma and Susi in England,** see Horace Waller, ed., *The Last Journals of David Livingstone* (London: Harper & Brothers, 1875); "Hidden Histories of Black Geographers," *Royal Geographical Society.*

For the story of Rassul Galwan, see Ghulam Rassul Galwan, *Servant of Sahibs* (Cambridge: W. Heffer, 1923). For a discussion of the production of Galwan's text and how such accounts of "Native Authenticity" could be leveraged for colonialist ends, see David Butz and Kenneth I. MacDonald, "Serving Sahibs with Pony and Pen: The Discursive Uses of 'Native Authenticity,'" *Environment and Planning D: Society and Space* 19 (2001): 179–201.

For more on exploration in the Himalayas, see Francis Younghusband, *The Heart of a Continent* (London: John Murray, 1896); Indra Singh Rawat, *Indian Explorers of the 19th Century* (New Delhi: Publications Division, Govt. of India, 1973); Peter Hopkirk, *Trespassers on the Roof of the World: The Race for Lhasa* (Oxford: Oxford University Press, 1982); Derek Waller, *The Pundits: British Exploration of Tibet and Central Asia* (Lexington: University Press of Kentucky, 1990); Peter Frankopan, *Silk Roads*, 265–311.

For Francis Younghusband's quotes on Galwan and other Indigenous Central Asian explorers, see Younghusband, *The Heart of a Continent*, 1.

On Younghusband and Ma-te-la, see Patrick French, *Younghusband: The Last Great Imperial Adventurer* (London: HarperCollins, 1994), 47.

On Roy Chapman Andrews, see Roy Chapman Andrews, *Whale Hunting with Gun and Camera* (New York: D. Appleton, 1916); Roy Chapman Andrews, *This Business of Exploring* (New York, 1935); Roy Chapman Andrews, *Under a Lucky Star: A Lifetime of Adventure* (New York: Viking, 1943); Charles Gallenkamp, *Dragon Hunter: Roy Chapman Andrews and the Central Asiatic Expeditions* (New York: Viking, 2001), 3, 53.

On the pundits and Indigenous explorations, see "Presentation of the Royal and Other Awards," *Proceedings of the Royal Geographical Society of London* 21, no. 5 (July 23, 1877): 397–403; Rudyard Kipling, *Kim* (New York: Oxford University Press, 1987), 222.

CHAPTER 6: MIGRATION

For Mary Antin's narrative, see Ronald Sanders, *Shores of Refuge: A Hundred Years of Jewish Emigration* (New York: Schocken, 1989), 156, 158–59, 160.

For Allyson Williams and the Windrush generation, see David Matthews, *Voices of the Windrush Generation: The Real Story Told by the People Themselves* (London: Blink, 2018), 122–58.

For the Anne Sofie Beck Knudsen study of immigration and individualism, see Anne Sofie Beck Knudsen, "Those Who Stayed: Individualism, Self-Selection and Cultural Change during the Age of Mass Migration," Social Science Research Network (SSRN), January 24, 2019.

For the stories of Mexican migrants, see Marilyn Davis, *Mexican Voices/American Dreams: An Oral History of Mexican Immigration to the United States* (New York: Holt, 1991), 15–16, 36–37, 117–22.

CONCLUSION: CONNECTION

For the story of Matthew Henson and the Robert Peary polar expedition, see Matthew Henson, "The Negro at the North Pole," *The World's Work* 19 (April 1910); "Matt Henson, Who Reached Pole with Peary in 1909, Dies at 88," *New York Times*, March 10, 1955; S. Allen Counter, *North Pole Legacy: Black, White, and Eskimo* (Amherst: University of Massachusetts Press, 1991).

For the ancestors of Matthew Henson and the anniversary commemorations, see Counter, *North Pole Legacy*; Jane George, "Matthew Henson's Descendants Honor Their Ancestor," *Nunatsiaq News*, April 9, 2009. For the controversy over the Peary expedition's claim to be the first to reach the North Pole, see Darrell Hartman, *Battle of Ink and Ice: A Sensational Story of News Barons, North Pole Explorers, and the Making of Modern Media* (New York: Viking, 2023).

INDEX

Page numbers in *italics* refer to illustrations.

Norton Shorts

BRILLIANCE WITH BREVITY

W. W. Norton & Company has been independent since 1923, when William Warder Norton and Mary (Polly) D. Herter Norton first published lectures delivered at the People's Institute, the adult education division of New York City's Cooper Union. In the 1950s, Polly Norton transferred control of the company to its employees.

One hundred years after its founding, W. W. Norton & Company inaugurates a new century of visionary independent publishing with Norton Shorts. Written by leading-edge scholars, these eye-opening books deliver bold thinking and fresh perspectives in under two hundred pages.

Available Fall 2024

Imagination: A Manifesto by Ruha Benjamin

Offshore: Stealth Wealth and the New Colonialism by Brooke Harrington

Explorers: A New History by Matthew Lockwood

Wild Girls: How the Outdoors Shaped the Women Who Challenged a Nation by Tiya Miles

Against Technoableism: Rethinking Who Needs Improvement by Ashley Shew

Literary Theory for Robots: How Computers Learned to Write by Dennis Yi Tenen

Forthcoming

Mehrsa Baradaran on the racial wealth gap

Rina Bliss on the "reality" of race

Merlin Chowkwanyun on the social determinants of health

Daniel Aldana Cohen on eco-apartheid

Jim Downs on cultural healing

Reginald K. Ellis on Black education versus Black freedom

Nicole Eustace on settler colonialism

Agustín Fuentes on human nature

Brooke Harrington on offshore finance

Justene Hill Edwards on the history of inequality in America

Destin Jenkins on a short history of debt

Quill Kukla on a new vision of consent

Barry Lam on discretion

Kelly Lytle Hernández on the immigration regime in America

Natalia Molina on the myth of assimilation

Rhacel Salazar Parreñas on human trafficking

Tony Perry on water in African American culture and history

Beth Piatote on living with history

Ashanté Reese on the transformative possibilities of food

Jeff Sebo on the moral circle

Tracy K. Smith on poetry in an age of technology

Daniel Steinmetz-Jenkins on religion and populism

Onaje X. O. Woodbine on transcendence in sports